The Day
After Midnight

The Day After Midnight

The Effects of Nuclear War

Based on a report by the
Office of Technology Assessment

Edited by Michael Riordan

CHESHIRE BOOKS • Palo Alto, California

Printed in the United States of America

Published by Cheshire Books, Inc.
514 Bryant Street, Palo Alto, CA 94301

Distributed in the United States by Kampmann & Company, Inc.
9 East 40th Street, New York, NY 10028

Distributed in Canada by Firefly Books, Ltd.
3520 Pharmacy Avenue, Unit 1C, Scarborough, Ontario M1W 2T8

Library of Congress Catalog Card Number 82-9538
10   9   8   7   6   5   4   3   2   1

Library of Congress Cataloging in Publication Data

Main entry under title:
The day after midnight.

    Based on: The effects of nuclear war.
    Washington: Congress of the U.S., Office of
Technology Assessment, 1979.
    Bibliography: p. 130
    Includes index.
    1. Atomic warfare. I. Riordan, Michael.
II. United States. Congress. Office of
Technology Assessment. The effects of nuclear war.

UF767.D38 1982   355'.0217   82-9538
ISBN 0-917352-11-4 (pbk.)

Acknowledgements

The Day After Midnight is based almost entirely on a report entitled "The Effects of Nuclear War," published in 1979 by the Office of Technology Assessment (OTA), United States Congress. The original text has been modified in a number of respects by Michael Riordan and his assistants. The people and institutions that prepared the original report are listed below in acknowledgement of the fact that this book would not have been possible without the analysis performed by OTA. The publisher wishes to thank them all for their contributions.

NUCLEAR WAR EFFECTS PROJECT STAFF

Lionel S. Johns, Assistant Director, OTA
Peter Sharfman, Project Director
Jonathan Medalia, Congressional Research Service
Robert W. Vining, Systems Science and Software
Kevin Lewis
Gloria Proctor
Henry Kelly
Marvin Ott

CONTRACTORS AND CONSULTANTS

Advanced Research and Applications Corporation
Analytical Assessments Corporation
General Research Corporation
Santa Fe Corporation
Systems Science and Software
Stuart Goldman
Nan Randall
George R. Rodericks
Ronald Stivers

NUCLEAR WAR EFFECTS PROJECT ADVISORY PANEL

David S. Saxon, Chairman

Donald G. Brennan	J. Carson Mark
Charles Cooper	James V. Neel
Russell E. Dougherty	Jack Ruina
Sidney Drell	Harriet Scott
Richard Garwin	Huston Smith
Gene R. LaRocque	John Steinbruner
Cecil Leith	Jeremy Stone
J. David Linebaugh	Hilary Whitaker

The Advisory Panel provided much advice and constructive criticism throughout the original Nuclear War Effects Project. The Panel did not, however, necessarily approve, disapprove, or endorse the original report. The Office of Technology Assessment is in no way responsible for—nor does it necessarily approve of—any differences between this book and the original OTA report.

To the village square we must carry the facts of atomic energy.
From there must come America's voice.

Albert Einstein

Contents

List of Figures

List of Tables

Foreword

In the waning decades of this century, we live with the looming peril that nuclear power may suddenly be turned against humanity in a catastrophe of terrifying proportions. Already we have witnessed two small samples of this ultimate catastrophe—Hiroshima and Nagasaki. But the atomic bombs that obliterated those two Japanese cities were crude weapons by today's megaton standards; their effects were largely confined within city limits. Modern thermonuclear devices can have global impacts, and the United States and Soviet Union have tens of thousands of these weapons. Thus, we are confronted today by the very real possibility that nuclear war may well end humanity's tenure on this planet.

The likely consequences of nuclear war have recently become a matter of considerable public debate. At one extreme, characterized by Jonathan Schell's eloquent book, *The Fate of the Earth*, nuclear devastation would be total and irreversible. The resulting breakdown of the Earth's ozone layer would be the final ecological insult causing widespread extinction of almost all higher life forms—leading, in Schell's memorable phrase, to a "republic of insects and grass." Others contend that an all-out nuclear war *is* survivable, if only we are adequately prepared. Though the carnage would far exceed that of all previous wars, some pockets of humanity would allegedly survive to rebuild society from the ruins of a post-nuclear world. Still others consider "limited" nuclear war—in which only military and economic tar-

gets, not population centers, are attacked—a possible occurrence that the country should include in its strategic planning. They presume that our leaders will have the "wisdom" (and technical capability) to refrain from an all-out nuclear "exchange" once the missiles have begun to fly.

The Day After Midnight is an important contribution to this nuclear weapons debate. Based on a widely circulated government report, "The Effects of Nuclear War" by the Congressional Office of Technology Assessment (OTA), it depicts in graphic detail the likely social and economic effects of nuclear war on both the United States and the Soviet Union. The book does not try to assess the probability that nuclear conflict, once initiated, would escalate into an all-out war. Rather, it examines four militarily plausible nuclear attack scenarios ranging from single weapons detonations to all-out, massive attacks. The one consistent conclusion in all cases is that nuclear war would be an unmitigated catastrophe unlike anything the world has ever experienced. The inherent uncertainties in these analyses—including the possibility of unbridled escalation—are tremendous. Thus, the total extinction of humanity cannot be completely ruled out.

Whereas the original OTA report was written primarily for government insiders, this book version has been edited and adapted for general readers interested in the issues of nuclear warfare. Sections relevant only to internal government debates have been removed. The book has also been reorganized to bring forth the more human elements of the original report. It is nearly impossible to convey the human and psychological effects of nuclear war—the misery, starvation and hopelessness that would inevitably ensue—in the abstract, statistical language of the original document. As partial remedy, a fictional account of the aftermath of a massive Soviet attack, originally included as an appendix to the OTA report, has been rewritten and included here as the opening chapter.

I do not agree with all the conclusions presented in the OTA report. But it is certainly a sober, well-reasoned analysis of the human and social consequences of nuclear war. Thus, I feel impelled to publish it for the larger audience of average readers eager to learn more about the most pressing issue of our time. Any material differences between *The Day After Midnight* and the original document are my sole responsibility.

No publication of this depth is ever the work of one person, and there are consequently many people to acknowledge in the present case. I wish to thank John C. Holmes, the OTA Publishing Officer, and his excellent staff for all their timely and courteous assistance in providing me the necessary materials and information. Dr. Peter Sharfman, the OTA Nuclear War Effects Project Director, reviewed my edited version and helped me correct a number of unwitting errors. My special thanks must go to Dr. Sidney Drell of Stanford University, a member of the Project Advisory Panel, who encouraged me to undertake this revision and provided valuable suggestions about how we might alter the OTA report for a general readership. An unsung heroine of the OTA project, in my mind, was consultant Nan Randall, whose disturbing fictional account was hidden in an appendix to the report; a revised version of that account opens this book. To her, and to all the other fine people involved in the Nuclear War Effects Project, I give my deepest thanks for their perseverance in a difficult task.

In preparing a book from the original OTA document, three people were most helpful, working cheerfully against deadlines no editor had any right to impose. R.G. Beukers was much more than a meticulous copy editor and proofreader; his imaginative changes and his inspired revision of Nan Randall's account helped humanize an otherwise stiff and formal book. With her perceptive designs, Wendy Calmenson unified the many disparate elements of an unwieldly government report into a coherent whole. Meredith Ittner, Cheshire Books' Production Manager, valiantly tried to keep all editorial and production activities on schedule; her persistence made a 1982 publication date possible. Finally, I appreciate the support, advice and guidance provided by my wife and partner, Linda Goodman, in all aspects of this publishing project.

The decisions that brought nuclear weapons into the world in such terrifying numbers have been made in secret by a few very powerful men. In contrast to this obsessive secrecy, the worldwide public attention now being focussed on the issues of nuclear war comes as a welcome breath of fresh air. Public education about the likely consequences of nuclear war is essential if people are to react to this threat in an intelligent manner. It is my fervent hope that this disturbing book will help us all realize the folly of nuclear weapons and find a way to remove them from this fragile planet.

Michael Riordan
Palo Alto, California
May, 1982

The Day After Midnight

1

Charlottesville: 1984

The last strand of peaceful coexistence snapped during the bitter winter of 1984, plunging the United States and the Soviet Union into a nuclear nightmare from which the world has yet to awaken. On January 8 of that year, nuclear warheads totalling more than 4,000 megatons destroyed military and industrial targets in the United States, killing close to 100 million people. Destruction ranged from the large industrial centers on the coasts and Great Lakes to small farming communities close to the great missile silos and military bases. The Northeast Corridor, from north of Boston to south of Norfolk, was reduced to a swath of burning rubble. The U.S. counterattack had a similar, devastating effect on the Soviet Union.

Still, there were some, mostly rural, areas that were spared the direct effects of blast and fire. Small, gracious Charlottesville, the elegant center of learning, culture, and trade in central Virginia, was not hit. At first it seemed like a miracle. No fireball had seared the city, no blast wave had crumpled buildings and buried the inhabitants, and no dark mushroom cloud had spread over the sky. A monument to the mind and manner of Jefferson, Charlottesville kept its former status as a kind of genteel sanctuary, momentarily immune from the disaster that had leveled other U.S. cities.

Editor's note: This fictional account was written by Nan Randall for the original OTA report and revised by R.G. Beukers for this book. Any similarity between actual persons and the characters herein is purely coincidental.

The nuclear attack did not come as a complete surprise. For some weeks, there had been mounting anxiety as radio and television reported deteriorating relations between the superpowers. The threat of possible nuclear war hung heavy in people's minds. As evidence reached the President's desk that a sizable number of Americans were deserting the major cities for the imagined safety of rural areas, he considered ordering a general evacuation. But, with the concurrence of his advisors, he decided that an evacuation call would be premature, and possibly provocative. There was no hard evidence that the Soviets were evacuating, and there was a good chance that the crisis would pass.

But spontaneous evacuation grew and spread. A week before the attack, Charlottesville had no free hotel or motel rooms. A few evacuees found lodgings with private families, but most were forced to camp by their cars in their trailers next to the fast-food chains on Route 29. The governing bodies of Charlottesville and surrounding Albemarle County were rumored to be concerned about the drain on the area's resources. "If this keeps up," remarked Alice Simms of the Board of Supervisors, "we're going to be overrun without any war."

Refugees came from Washington, 100 miles to the northeast and from Richmond, 70 miles to the southeast. A few of the hardier types continued on into the Blue Ridge Mountains and the caverns near Skyline Drive; the majority sought the reassurances of civilization that the small city could provide.

The population of Charlottesville normally stood a little above 40,000, while Albemarle County boasted an additional 40,000 to 50,000. With the arrival of the evacuees, the combined population was well over 120,000.

In the week before the attack, much of the population familiarized itself with the location of fallout shelters. Little hoarding took place as retailers limited sales of food and other necessities. Both adults and children carried transistor radios when they were away from home. But most of the residents of Charlottesville continued to live as they always had, although they were particularly alert for sirens or bulletin broadcasts on the radio. Many children stayed out of school.

At the sound of the sirens and the emergency radio alerts, most of the people hurried to shelter. Fortunately, Charlottesville had a surplus of shelter space for its own population, though the refugees easily took up the slack. Many headed for the University of Virginia and the basements of the old neoclassical buildings designed by Thomas Jefferson; others headed downtown for the office building parking garages. Carrying a few personal effects, blankets, transistor radios, and cans and bottles of food, they converged in a quiet if unordered mass. For most people, the obvious emotional crises — grief at leaving behind a pet, anxiety at being unable to locate a family member or relative — were suppressed by the overwhelming fear of the impending attack.

Some residents chose not to join the group shelters. Many suburbanites had ample, sturdy basements and food stocks. They preferred not to crowd themselves. Those who had taken the precaution of piling dirt against the windows and doors of their basements found that they provided adequate shelter. Among the rural poor, there was a reluctance to desert the small farms that represented the sum of their life's work. They wondered whether, if they left, they would return to find their means of livelihood gone. Further, many lived far from an adequate public shelter. So they stayed.

Most did not see the attacks on Richmond and Washington as they huddled in their shelters. But the sky to the east of Charlottesville glowed brilliantly in the noonday sun. At first no one knew how extensive the damage was. Communication nationwide was interrupted as the Earth's atmosphere shivered with the assault of the explosions. Each town, city, village, or farm was an island forced to suffer its fate alone.

An hour after the attacks subsided, rescue squads and police were dispatched to scour the countryside for stragglers to get them to shelters. Even if the population was safe from the direct effects of nuclear warheads, another danger was imminent. Fallout, the deadly cloud of radioactive particles sucked up by the nuclear fireballs, could easily blanket the town in a matter of hours. No one could predict how much fallout there would be or where it would go. It could poison many of those idyllic rural towns and villages that seemed light-years away from the problems of international power and politics. Fortunately for Charlottesville, the University of Virginia and the hospitals had sophisticated radiological monitoring equipment, and the training to use it. Many other towns were not so lucky.

Two hours after the attack warnings had sounded, the nuclear engineering staff detected the first fallout. Starting at a moderate level of about 40 rems an hour — a cumulative dose of 450 rems received in a 1 week period is fatal to half of those exposed — the intensity soon rose to 50 rems an hour. The total dose in the first 4 days was 2,000 rems, which killed everybody who refused to believe shelter was necessary and increased the risk of eventually dying of cancer for those who were properly sheltered. For the immediate period, it was essential to stay as protected as possible.

For several days, Charlottesville remained immobile, suspended in time. It was unclear just what had happened or would happen. The President delivered a message of encouragement, which was carried by those emergency radio stations that could still broadcast. As the atmosphere cleared, radio station WCHV was able to transmit sporadically on its backup transmitter and emergency generator in the basement. However, the message from the President posed more questions than it answered — the damage assessment was incomplete. Nevertheless, he said that there was a tentative cease-fire.

In the first days of sheltering, only those with some particular expertise had much to do. Nuclear engineers and technicians from the university monitored radiation in the shelters they occupied, and CB radios broadcast results to other shelters. Doctors attempted to treat physical and psychological ailments — the symptoms of radiation sickness, flu, and acute anxiety being unnervingly similar — while police and government officials tried to keep order. The rest waited.

For the time being, the food stocks brought to the shelter were adequate if not appetizing. The only problem was the water supply, which was contaminated with radioactive Iodine 131. Potassium iodide pills available in some shelters provided protection; elsewhere people drank bottled water, or as little water as possible.

Not all shelters had enough food and other necessities. Most shelters had no toilets. The use of trash cans for human waste was an imperfect system, and several days into the shelter period, the stench was overpowering. Because many suffered from diarrhea — the result of anxiety, flu, or radiation sickness — the lack of toilet facilities was especially difficult.

But shelter life was not without its comforts, especially in the beginning. Communications by CB radio allowed some shelters to communicate with one another, to locate missing family members and friends. A genuine altruism or community spirit of cooperation was present in almost all the shelters — though some of them were fairly primitive. Even those out-of-town refugees who were crowded into halls and basements with the local residents were welcomed. Parents kept an eye on one another's children or shared scarce baby food. Shelter residents felt a sense of relief. They believed themselves to be among the lucky ones of this world. They had survived.

Within a few days, an emergency radio station was able to broadcast quite regularly. There were occasional interruptions, though, because the ionosphere does not clear all at once. The station had had no protection from the electromagnetic pulse that can shatter the inner workings of electronic equipment during a nuclear explosion. However, by detaching the backup transmitter at the sound of the warning, Ralph Palmer, the station engineer, had protected his equipment. Intermittent communications from Emergency Operations Centers got through to Charlottesville officials, though the main communications center at Olney, Maryland was silent. Telephone switching facilities were almost entirely out, although the small, independent phone company would be operational fairly quickly.

Lifeline of the sheltered community was the CB radio. Rural Virginians had been CB fans long before it became a national craze, and they put their equipment to imaginative use when it became clear that Ma Bell's coast-to-coast trunk lines might take a year or more to reconnect. Prodded by anxious refugees and local residents who had relatives and friends in other parts of the world, CBers tried to set up a relay system along the lines of an electronic pony express. Though less than perfect, the CB relay was able to bring limited news from outside, most of the news being acutely distressing. Little was left of the coastal cities. Those who had abandoned family or friends to come to Charlottesville understood that probably they would never see them again. The first surge of grief swept over the refugees and those Charlottesville residents who were affected. In time, the sorrow of loss would affect almost everyone.

Three days after the attacks, a large influx of refugees poured into Charlottesville, many of them suffering with early symptoms of radiation sickness. They had been caught poorly sheltered or too close to the nuclear targets. A few showed the effects of blast and fire, bringing home to Charlottesville the tangible evidence of the war's destruction. Some refugees had driven, while others had hitchhiked or even walked, to reach what they hoped was safety and medical help. On the way, many were forced to abandon those who were too weak to continue.

The hospitals were completely overwhelmed. Up to now, they had managed to treat the ill with a modicum of order. Patients' beds had been moved to interior corridors for fallout protection; emergency surgery was feasible with diesel generators; hospital staff slept in the most protected areas. Some borderline cases in intensive care were allowed to die, and any elective medical procedures were eliminated. Still, hospitals were able to cope, even with the increasing number of common ailments caused by the shelter crowding.

But suddenly this changed. Fallout levels were too high for anyone to be out in the open for any length of time, but the people came anyway. The carefully laid plans of the University of Virginia Emergency Room, devised for the possibility of peacetime accidents, were hurriedly modified.

No longer was the careful showering and decontaminating of victims possible with the single shower and uncertain water pressure. Instead, patients were stripped of their clothes and issued hospital gowns. With no time for studied decision, doctors segregated the very sick from the moderately sick—the latter to be treated, the former given medication and allowed to die.

Soon the hospitals were full. The University Hospital, Martha Jefferson Hospital, the Blue Ridge Sanatorium, and the others were forced to lock their doors to protect those patients they had already accepted.

After being turned away, the sick had no specific destination. Many still clustered around the middle of town near the two major hospitals, taking up residence in the houses abandoned by local residents several days before. With minimal protection from fallout and no medical treatment for other trauma, many died, their bodies left unburied for several weeks.

The population of Charlottesville nearly doubled in the seven days after the nuclear attack. Slowly, hostility and resentment wedged a gap between residents and refugees who attempted to join the group shelters. The refugees, still in a daze from their experience, believed that they had priority rights after all they had suffered. The local residents viewed the outsiders as a threat to their own survival, particularly as the extent of the war damage became evident.

However the supply of food was not a problem in the short run. Like most other towns and cities, Charlottesville had some three weeks worth of food in homes, supermarkets and wholesale outlets. The Morton Frozen Food plant would supply a rich diet of convenience foods for a short time, even though the refrigeration failed when distant sources of electricity were destroyed. But after local food supplies were exhausted, where could more be obtained?

Nerves, already raw from the stresses of a week with no end in sight, threatened to disintegrate. Older people were bothered by the noise and commotion of children; children resented the lack of freedom. Friction between differing groups increased to the level of outright hostility. An experiment in communal living was clearly not to the taste of many, and physical and psychological discomforts forced local residents out of the shelters. Because radiation levels still posed some hazards, these people were urged to stay inside their homes most of the time. Left in the shelters, now, were mostly those out-of-town refugees who had no homes to go to.

Not all residents of Charlottesville found their homes intact. Some houses had been looted or occupied by refugees who were unwilling to give up squatters' rights. Sometimes claims were backed with guns; in a few cases, squatter and owner worked out an agreement to share the property.

Farm animals confined to fairly solid barns with uncontaminated feed had a fair chance of surviving. Many of these animals, however, were missing, apparently eaten by hungry refugees and residents. Some pets had remained indoors in good de facto shelters so that, if they had found water, they needed only to be fed to regain health. Worried about the amount of food pets could consume, many families put them out to fend for themselves.

For the first week or so after the nuclear attacks, local authorities had few options. The main priority of this generally ad hoc government was survival, the elements of which included food and water distribution, fallout protection, and retention of some civil order. As the population left the shelters, officials felt that some formal system of emergency government was desirable. After several long meetings — in the basement of the courthouse where the government officials had stayed to avoid fallout — a new system of government, led by city manager Dan Green was formed. The chairman of the County Board of Supervisors, Jim Tate, was named his deputy, and Sheriff Robeson was made chief of public safety to oversee the police forces and provide liaison with military units still in the area.

The powers given to Green — an energetic optimist who would rather run up several flights of stairs than take the elevator to his third-floor office — were sweeping in scope, certainly far beyond any powers he had held before. While some considered the new form of local government close to martial law, great care was exercised to be sure that the offensive term was not used. In effect, however, the entire county was under a highly centralized, almost totalitarian rule, and Green was the closest thing to a benevolent dictator that Charlottesville had ever seen.

Under the new system, he took over the allocation of all resources. However, he soon became painfully aware that his government was not set up to "go it alone" without any outside help. Charlottesville was no longer an agricultural center. There wasn't enough energy to process any food that might be grown. Where would people get clothes and building materials and medicines and spare parts? The very complexity of American society — its technological marvels and high standard of living — could well prove to be a barrier to reconstruction.

During the third week after the attacks, Green introduced the new rationing system. Individual identification cards were issued to every man, woman, and child. Food was distributed at centralized points. Those without I.D. cards were unable to get their ration of flour, powdered milk, and lard — and the processing of cards could take three or more days. Some desperate refugees resorted to stealing I.D. cards to get food, while an enterprising printer started turning out forgeries. Hoarding and black marketeering abounded. Missing supermarket food turned up in black market centers, accompanied by exhorbitant prices.

Fuel supplies dropped more rapidly than Green had hoped. Most families heated their homes with wood, either in fireplaces or in oil drums recycled for stoves. As winter waned, fuel was desperately needed for driving motors and generators. Drinking water, for example, was dependent on an emergency generator that drove a single purifying system for the Rivanna Water and Sewer Authority. The hospital and radio stations also ran on small generators. The University could luxuriate in its coal-powered steam heat, but only generators could power electric lights.

No one knew for sure how much fuel was left in the area. For emergency planning purposes, the city had once surveyed its fuel storage capacity, and Green hoped he could count on having about half of that on hand. He assigned armed guards to large facilities that had not yet been siphoned dry by the desperate. He also outlawed all private use of cars or tractors and threatened to confiscate any moving vehicles.

Two weeks after the attack, major utilities were far from recovery. But limited electricity from the small Bremo Bluff power plant 15 miles away become available for a few hours each day. This was particularly pleasant for those families whose water came from electrical well-pumps. Well water was issued to children for drinking because it had escaped the Iodine 131 contamination that was still present in the reservoirs.

After two weeks the radiation level dropped to 0.4 rem per hour and it was "safe" to go outdoors. However, the resulting doses, though too low to cause immediate illness or deaths, posed a long-term health hazard. Recognizing that everybody would receive many times the prewar "safe dose," the authorities tried to reduce the hazards by urging people to stay inside as much as possible when not picking up food rations at the distribution centers. Life for the residents of Charlottesville revolved around those trips and finding ways to make do without normal supplies and services. Some chanced outings to forage for a greater variety of food, but most were resigned to waiting. There wasn't much else they could do.

———————

Three weeks after the nuclear attack, most Charlottesville residents had returned to their homes except for those whose homes had been occupied by squatters or destroyed by fire. As for the refugees, the drop in fallout intensity allowed them to move out of basements and interior halls, but they were still forced to live a version of camp life. They spent their endless, empty hours waiting in lines for food, for a chance to use the bathrooms, or for a chance to request preferential treatment from Dan Green's assistant. Information from the outside was still sketchy, and this uncertainty added to their high level of anxiety.

Green and his emergency government tried to solve the refugee housing problem by billeting them in private homes. At first he asked for volunteers, but got few. He then announced that any house with fewer than two people per room would be assigned a refugee family. Resistance to this order was strong. In outlying areas that were hard to check, outright defiance was common. Families pretended to comply and then forced the refugees out as soon as the authorities left. The refugees struggled back to town, or took up residence in barns or garages.

Still more refugees came to Charlottesville, bringing stories of the horrors they had experienced. They camped in schools, in banks, in warehouses. By night the neoclassical architecture of the university was packed with the people from Arlington and Alexandria. By day, the new downtown mall was awash with a floating mass of men, women, and children, who, with nothing to do, milled around the unopened stores. Ray Field, a retired U.S. ambassador to India, was overheard comparing the scene to that of downtown Calcutta.

Green and his government saw that the need for food was soon going to be acute. Without power for refrigeration, much food had spoiled. Stocks of nonperishable foods were mostly exhausted. As shortages became clear, the price of food skyrocketed. Many people refused money in exchange for food, preferring instead to barter. Food and fuel were the most valuable commodities, with shoes and coats high on the list.

Since shortly after the attack, Green had been in contact with both the federal and state officials. He had repeatedly asked for emergency rations, only to receive vague promises and explanations about the problems of transportation. He was generally urged to cut rations further and hang on. Help would arrive when it could.

For some time, the few surviving farm animals had been disappearing. The farmers concluded that "those damned city folks" were stealing them for food, although some of the local residents were also making midnight forays on the livestock. Farmers themselves slaughtered animals they had planned to fatten up for the future. They couldn't spare the feed grain, and they needed food now.

Finally, Green announced that the emergency authorities would take a percentage of every farmer's livestock to help feed residents and refugees. Farmers were outraged, considering the action simple theft. Angry farmers shot several agents who tried to confiscate the animals. Farmers were offered promissory notes from the city, but they considered such payment worthless.

Radiological experts at the university were questioned on the advisability of eating the meat of animals with radiation sickness. Many beasts that had remained outside during the high fallout period were showing severe symptoms of radiation sickness, such as bleeding sores and hair falling out. The experts decided that the meat would be edible if cooked sufficiently to kill any bacterial invasion — a result of the deterioration of the animal's digestive tract. Strontium 90 would be concentrated in the bones or the milk, not the muscle tissue.

Three weeks after the attack, the President made a major address to reassure the people. He announced that the cease-fire was still holding and he saw no reason why that would change. He described the damage that the U.S. retaliatory strike had done to the Soviet Union. He also noted that the United States still retained enough nuclear weapons, most of them at sea on submarines, to inflict considerable damage on any nation that attempted to take advantage of the recent past. He did not mention that the Soviets also held reserve weapons.

Describing the damage that the country had suffered, the President noted that, even with the loss of over 100 million lives, "We still have reserves, both material and spiritual, unlike any nation on earth." He asked for patience and for prayers.

There had been broadcasts earlier by Richard Duke, the Governor of Virginia, from his shelter in Roanoke. However, as fallout in the Roanoke area was quite high (Radford just to the west had been struck), he was effectively immobilized for some time.

Charlottesville was still on its own. Her inhabitants hunted game as the last of the food stocks disappeared, but the fallout had killed most animals living in the open. Many people resorted to stealing. A number of people managed to fill their gas tanks with contraband gasoline and set out to forage in the Blue Ridge Mountains.

Three and one-half weeks after the attack, an old propeller-driven cargo plane landed at Charlottesville Airport with a supply of flour, powdered milk, and vegetable oil. The pilot assured the few policemen who guarded the airstrip that more would be on the way by truck as soon as temporary bridges could be built over the major rivers.

The emergency airlift was supposed to supply Charlottesville with food for a week or two. However, the officials who had calculated the allotment had overlooked the refugees. The city's population had tripled by now, although no one was absolutely sure of this because the refugees moved around a great deal from camp to camp.

The first of the radiation deaths occurred ten days after the attack, and the number grew steadily. Now it was common to see mass funerals several times a day. Hospitals provided no care for the terminally ill. There were too many, and there was little that could be done for them anyway, so it was up to their families to do what they could. Fortunately there were still ample supplies of morphine, and college students donated marijuana. Dan Green had the city set aside several locations for mass graves on the outskirts of town.

There were also people with nonfatal cases of radiation sickness. Often it was impossible for doctors to quickly identify those with flu or psychosomatic radiation symptoms. The number of patients crowding the emergency rooms did not slacken off. The refugees, crowded together, passed a variety of common disorders, from colds to diarrhea, back and forth. Public health experts worried about an outbreak of infectious diseases like measles or even polio. "So far, we have been lucky not to have a major epidemic of typhus or cholera," observed one doctor.

Hospital drug supplies were dwindling fast. Although penicillin could be manufactured fairly easily in university laboratories, it had to be administered with large veterinary hypodermics because the homemade mix was too coarse for the small disposable hypos that most doctors stocked. There was a considerable shortage of the larger needles. And medications other than penicillin were in such short supply that many patients with chronic illnesses such as heart disease, kidney failure, and diabetes died within a few weeks.

Food riots — precipitated by the first large shipment of grain — broke out in mid-February. Three large tractor-trailers pulled into the parking lot of the Citizens Commonwealth Building quite unexpectedly. The trucks were greeted with cheers until the residents of Charlottesville discovered that they contained raw grain instead of flour. The drivers were taken unawares when they were showered with empty cans and bottles. One driver jumped in his cab and departed before his truck could be unloaded.

Because few people knew what to do with raw grain, a number of angry citizens broke open the sacks and scattered wheat through the parking lot. They in turn were set upon by those who wanted to conserve as much as possible. The city's finest waded into the melee with night sticks and tear gas.

Later, Dan Green had to explain that "processed food is going to those areas where most of the people are sick or injured." Also, those in charge of distributing the grain assumed that the Charlottesville area still had livestock to feed. But everyone blamed everyone else for the incident, and the fragile glue that had held public order together began to dissolve.

From this time on, it was almost impossible for Green and other local authorities to convince everyone they were getting a fair share. People in one section of town would watch suspiciously as delivery trucks passed them by and headed somewhere else. Blacks distrusted whites, the poor distrusted the rich, and everyone distrusted the refugees as "outsiders."

The refugees were convinced that the local authorities were favoring the residents and tried repeatedly to get state intervention, with little success. The refugee camps were a breeding ground for discontent and even rebellion.

Activities at the federal level were not entirely confined to radio broadcasts or the occasional delivery of food. The government put out calls for volunteers to help the National Guard dig out cities and start reconstruction, but found that most workers, young and old, wanted to stay with their families. A system of national conscription for young men and women with no children was in the planning stage.

The federal government also urged people to return to their cities and help rebuild them — an activity that would also redistribute the population to a more normal pattern. Some refugees were happy to attempt to return, particularly those whose houses were more or less intact. However, those who found their homes destroyed preferred to return to the refugee camps. There was nothing to hold them to their former lives. Fearful memories of the past made any time spent in the cities painful.

One day in early March, quite without warning, Dan Green was informed that half of his fuel stores would be confiscated by the federal government, for the military and for the reconstruction effort. Earth-moving equipment was gathering on the outskirts of the devastated cities and needed fuel. When it was clear that there was no way to stop the government from taking the fuel, Green suggested that unmarked tank trucks, well guarded, pick up the stocks at night. He knew that knowledge of this action would further enrage and ultimately depress the people of Charlottesville.

Already transportation was nearly nonexistent. A sporadic bus service ran from one end of town to the other once a day, and an occasional school bus made a sortie out into the suburbs. With even less fuel available, the bus service would be cut in half. Bicycles were prized, and sometimes fought over. Those gentlemen farmers whose thoroughbred horses had been protected from fallout could use these animals for transportation, but it was risky to let the animals stand unprotected. Horse thievery had made an anachronistic reappearance.

———————

By mid-March, barter was clearly established as the preferred means of trade. For a time, the government paid for commandeered foodstuff and resources with checks and promissory notes, but no one wanted them anymore. Local banks—which had opened for a few days, only to find their customers lined up to withdraw everything—closed down. A few people hoarded money, but most thought it worthless. Stores either never opened or shut down quickly when they were overrun. Many stores had been looted in the second week after the attack, when the fallout intensity had dropped.

Workers in small industries in the Charlottesville area saw no point in turning up for work if all they could get was paper money. They preferred to spend their time hunting for food and fuel. If barter was a highly inefficient way to do business—it's hard to make change for a side of beef—it was still preferable to using worthless currency.

Psychologically, the population seemed to be in a quiet holding pattern. Many of the refugees had survived experiences that would mark them for years. Memories of fire, collapsing buildings, and screaming, trapped people were still vivid, and some refugees trembled at loud noises. However, profound grief over lost family, possessions, and friends made many people apathetic and passive. These victims of nuclear attack were also victims of its aftermath. Still shunned as outsiders by the resident population, most refugees accepted exclusion just as the surviving population of Hiroshima and Nagasaki had almost 40 years before.

Charlottesville residents were disoriented. For each one lucky enough to have a job, there were many unemployed. They turned inward to their families or friends. Their worries about the future—would there be another attack, would they go back to their old jobs—made most days anxious and unproductive. Children reflected a con-

tinuous nervousness picked up from their elders and had difficulty sleeping at night. Though many parents hoped for a return to normalcy once the schools reopened, others quietly decided not to send their children for fear of a second outbreak of war.

———————

Spring changed many things. A new optimism surfaced as everyone looked forward to planting, good weather, and warmth. The residents of Charlottesville had survived the first hurdle; they felt confident they could survive the next.

University agronomists studied the best crops to plant in the Charlottesville area. But no one knew what effect the nuclear explosions had had on the ozone layer. If the ozone was severely depleted, more ultraviolet rays could reach the crops and burn them — especially delicate crops such as peas and beans. Hence, the government recommended that hardier crops, such as potatoes and soybeans, be planted and that available fertilizer go to farmers who followed government guidelines.

Dan Green announced that two-thirds of the former pasture land surrounding Charlottesville was to be cultivated. Feed grains were to be used for humans, not livestock. Dairy cattle and chickens were the only exceptions.

The next few months had a slow, almost dreamlike quality. Fears of new attacks abated. It was a time of settling into a new lifestyle, a severely simplified way of being, of making do. Children rarely ate meat, cheese, or eggs; adults practically never. A good pair of shoes was guarded — and worn only when necessary. With warmer weather, most children and adults went barefoot, heightening medical concern about an increase in parasitic diseases such as hookworm.

Most people were unable to return to their former jobs. Some employers never reopened for business, their goods and services being irrelevant in the post-attack society. College teachers, for example, had no students to teach; computer programmers had no computers to program.

For some, it was relatively easy to adapt. Electronics experts set up CB and short-wave radio repair shops. Cottage industries — sandal and clothing manufacturing from recycled materials, soap and candle making — sprang up in many homes. Some workers quickly acquired relevant skills. Others had to make do with menial jobs — burying the dead, cleaning the streets, and assisting carpenters and bricklayers.

There were also those who could not fit in anywhere. Many found it difficult to adapt to the idleness. Disruption of the 9 to 5 work ethic was a disruption of basic psychological props, of a sense of identity. In the immediate period after the attacks, parents concentrated on protection of their families. Once their families were no longer in physical danger, adults were robbed of their traditional roles.

By now, some refugees had melted into the general population. But the vast majority were no further along than in the late winter. The drag on area resources was significant, and many officials suggested that Dan Green find a way to force them out.

Charlottesville was fortunate in many respects, however. Two easily repairable rail lines offered access to the outside world. Travel was only permitted with a special pass, though, so younger members of the community resorted to the hallowed art of riding the rods.

Federal officials, many of whom had frequently visited Charlottesville and the university in the past, kept in closer contact with the city than with many other locales. Residents undoubtedly benefitted from more government assistance. As a result, Charlottesville became the unofficial "capital" of the area, economically and politically.

But as autumn approached, a universal depression settled on the residents and refugees. Starvation had been held at bay by the planting — but crop yields were smaller than expected. The weather was still fine, but there seemed to be no appreciable progress towards pre-attack conditions. The momentum toward reconstruction slowed as the young men and women who had been conscripted to build housing for the nation's refugees returned with gloomy reports of widespread industrial devastation. The East Coast was

effectively leveled. Where factories were rebuildable, the shortage of materials precluded their operation.

Recognizing that many families would have to make do without heating oil or gas, the Agriculture Extension Service issued pamphlets on how to make wood-burning stoves. Fortunately for Charlottesville and the surrounding area, trees were plentiful.

————————————

The following winter was harder than anyone had expected. Few additional deaths could be directly attributed to nuclear blast effects or radiation, but much of the surviving population was sick in body, mind, and spirit. Lack of medicines, adequate food, and reasonable shelter, plus lingering physical and psychological effects, left many people unable to work effectively, even if work was available. Flu raged through the cities of the east where refugees were huddled in camps. Many died, especially children and old people. Although vaccine for this particular, common strain of flu had been developed, the stocks had been destroyed in the attack.

In the northern sections of the country, food supplies were inadequate and poorly distributed. The average diet — day in, day out — consisted of unleavened bread and potatoes, and shortages of these staples were commonplace. Because animal populations, both domestic and wild, had been decimated by fallout and indiscriminate hunting, meat generally came from dogs, cats, and rats — those animals whose living habits protected them from fallout. Diseases caused by dietary deficiencies appeared.

Next to food, the most severe shortage was housing. Even with the temporary barracks that had been erected in clusters around damaged cities, refugees were crowded two or three to a room. Kitchens were shared by four or five families; bathrooms by as many as twelve people. Growing children were the first to notice the lack of replacement clothes — particularly shoes. Coats and blankets were highly prized in the cold climates.

There was relatively little work to occupy time,

schooling was curtailed, if it existed at all, and there was very little entertainment to relieve the widespread misery. The "dream machines" of California and New York had been particularly hard hit. Local TV stations could broadcast and rebroadcast those old films and cartoons they had in stock, but little was distributed nationwide. In small towns, public libraries were overwhelmed. In large cities, the libraries had been destroyed. There were no movie houses to speak of and no professional sports.

In Charlottesville alone, several thousand people died in the first winter after the nuclear attack. It was a season so grim and discouraging that it made George Washington's long winter at Valley Forge seem like a brief sojourn by comparison. Now, instead of revolutionary birth pains, the nation was experiencing the death rattle of a declining civilization.

"After consultation with numerous experts and government officials throughout this smitten land, I no longer believe our decline to be reversible," confessed a morose Dan Green in his farewell address almost a year after he had assumed office. "The fabric of our society has been torn in so many places that it can't possibly be mended — not in my lifetime or the lifetime of anyone living."

"And because I'm no longer the optimist you placed in office — because I can no longer perceive or divine a direction that will foster a political life worth living — I'm retiring to whatever light and comfort can still be found in the bosom of my family."

As citizen Green descended the steps of city hall, he took them in a daze, one at a time, and gripped the handrail as though his legs might crumble beneath him.

2

Possible Nuclear Wars

Nuclear war is not a comfortable subject. Throughout all the variations, possibilities, and uncertainties presented in this book, there is one constant theme: a nuclear war would be an unmitigated catastrophe. Even a "limited" nuclear attack would kill and injure people and inflict economic damage on a scale unprecedented in American history. A large-scale nuclear exchange would be a calamity unprecedented in human experience. The mind may recoil from any effort to predict the details of such catastrophes; it may well avoid any careful explanation of the vast uncertainties involved in predicting them. But the fact remains that nuclear war *is* possible and has become more probable in recent years. Ignoring this possibility will not make it go away.

The possibility of nuclear war has been an important part of international politics, and of U.S. foreign policy, ever since nuclear weapons were first used in 1945. But for the past two decades nuclear war has been an issue almost exclusively reserved for government professionals and insiders. Only recently, with heightening world tensions and the failure of the Strategic Arms Limitation Talks (SALT), has the general public once again asked to participate in the decisions about nuclear weaponry.

The premise of this book is that people should be well informed about this highly controversial issue so they can make appropriate decisions. They should understand what is known, and not known, about the likely consequences of nuclear war. Such an informed public, it is hoped, should be able to make better decisions about the use and disposal of nuclear weapons.

Military projections commonly understate the destruction and human suffering resulting from an all-out nuclear attack. In addition to tens of millions of deaths during the days and weeks after the attack, there would probably be further millions (perhaps further tens of millions) of deaths in the ensuing months or years. In addition to the enormous destruction caused by the actual nuclear explosions, there would be years during which the residual economy would decline further, as stocks of supplies were consumed and machines wore out faster than they could be replaced. Industrial civilization might well collapse in the areas attacked. Areas spared the direct effects, like Charlottesville in the preceding account, would still have to struggle mightily to maintain even minimal levels of human health and economic activity.

The impact of even a "small" or "limited" nuclear attack would still be enormous. The Office of Technology Assessment (OTA) examined the impact of a "small" attack on oil refineries and found that while economic recovery would be possible, the economic damage and social dislocation would be immense. A review of other calculations of the effects of major counterforce attacks directed solely at military targets found that, while the consequences might be endurable, the number of civilian deaths might be as high as 20 million. And because of huge uncertainties, no government can predict with any confidence what the results of a limited attack or counterattack would be — even if there were no further escalation.

The effects of a nuclear war that cannot be calculated are at least as important as those that can. And even these limited calculations are subject to very large uncertainties. Military planners base their calculations on factors that can be either controlled or predicted; they make conservative assumptions where prediction is impossible. Thus, the actual damage is likely to be greater than that reflected in the military calculations — particularly in the case of indirect effects such as deaths resulting from injuries and the unavailability of medical care, or of economic damage resulting from disruption and disorganization. Extreme uncertainties about the civilian effects of

a nuclear attack, when coupled with the knowledge that the minimum consequences would be enormous, play a significant role in the deterrent effect of nuclear weapons.

There are major differences between the United States and the Soviet Union that affect their vulnerability to nuclear attacks, despite the fact that both are large and diversified industrial countries. Differences in population distribution, closeness of population to other targets, vulnerability of agricultural systems, vulnerability of cities to fire, economic system, and political system lead to large differences in the potential effects of nuclear attacks. Differences in civil defense preparations and in the structure of the strategic arsenals compound these asymmetries. The Soviet Union is favored by geography and by a political structure geared to emergencies; the United States is favored by having a bigger and better economy and perhaps a greater capacity for effective decentralization. The larger size of Soviet weapons means that they are likely to kill more people while aimed at a factory or military installation.

Although effective sheltering or evacuation could save lives, it is not certain that a civil defense program based on providing shelters or planning evacuation would necessarily be effective. To save lives, it is necessary to provide food, water, medical supplies, sanitation, security against other people, and possibly filtered air. After fallout diminishes, there must be enough supplies and organization to keep people alive while production is being restored. As the Charlottesville account indicated, this will rarely be the case. The effectiveness of civil defense measures depends, among other things, on the events leading up to the attack, the enemy's targeting policy, and sheer luck.

The situation in which the survivors of a nuclear attack find themselves will be quite unprecedented. The surviving nation would be far weaker — economically, socially, and politically — than one might calculate by adding up the surviving economic assets and the numbers and skills of the surviving people. Nuclear warfare destroys not just buildings and people but the entire infrastructure of an industrial society — the institutions and implicit assumptions that are essential to its effective functioning. Natural resources would be destroyed; surviving equipment would require materials and skills that might no longer exist; and some regions might be almost uninhabitable. Prewar patterns of behavior would surely change, though in unpredictable ways. Finally, the entire society would suffer from the enormous psychological shock of having discovered its drastic vulnerability.

From an economic viewpoint, and possibly from a political and social viewpoint as well, conditions after an attack would get worse before they started to get better. For a period of time, people could live off supplies (and, in a sense, off habits) left over from before the war. But shortages and uncertainties would get much worse. The survivors would find themselves in a race to achieve economic viability before stocks ran out completely. Failure to achieve viability, or even slow recovery, would result in many additional deaths and much additional deterioration. This postwar damage could be as devastating as the actual nuclear explosions.

THE PLAN OF THIS BOOK

This book is broader in scope than most studies of the effects of nuclear war. It considers a full range of possible nuclear attacks, with attack forces ranging from a single nuclear weapon to the bulk of each superpower's arsenal. It also considers Soviet attacks on the United States *and* U.S. attacks on the Soviet Union. Finally, it addresses the multiple effects of nuclear war — indirect as well as direct, long-term as well as short-term, and social and economic as well as physical. Those effects that cannot be estimated accurately are described qualitatively.

In one area this book is narrower in scope than most defense analyses: it explicitly avoids any consideration of the military effects of nuclear war. Although missile and bomber attacks against military targets are among the scenarios considered, only the "collateral" damage of such attacks on civilian society is examined. No attempt is made to assess the ability of either coun-

TABLE 1.   Summary of Cases

Case	Description
1	Attack on single city: Detroit and Leningrad; 1 weapon. or 10 small weapons.
2	Attack on oil refineries, limited to 10 missiles.
3	Counterforce attack; includes attack only on ICBM silos as a variant.
4	Attack on range of military and economic targets using large fraction of existing arsenal.

For each case, the first section describes a Soviet attack on the United States, and the following section a U.S. attack on the Soviet Union.

try to respond to an initial nuclear strike by the other.

The book considers a series of attack cases (Table 1) and describes the various effects and overall impact each of them might produce. By analyzing the impact of both a U.S. attack on the Soviet Union and a similar Soviet attack on the United States, it examines the significance of the different vulnerabilities of the two countries and the consequences of the differences between their nuclear weapon arsenals. The cases were chosen primarily to investigate the effects of variations in attack size and in the kinds of targets. The analysis is believed to be "realistic," in the sense that the hypothetical attacks are possible. The patterns of nuclear explosions examined are not very different from those that OTA believes existing nuclear forces would produce if the military were ordered to make attacks of the specified sizes on the targets selected (see Table 2).

Case 1. To provide a tutorial on what happens when nuclear weapons are detonated, Chapter 3 describes the effects of exploding a single weapon. Then it examines the effects of such an explosion over a single U.S. city (Detroit) and single Soviet city (Leningrad) of comparable size. The base case is the detonation of a 1 megaton weapon (1 Mt = energy released by one million tons of TNT), since both the United States and the Soviet Union have weapons of roughly this size in their arsenals. Then, the effects of a 25 Mt weapon over Detroit, a 9 Mt weapon over Leningrad, and 10 weapons of 40 kilotons (kt) each over Leningrad are described. Finally, an attempt was made to describe the effects of a small weapon — one that a terrorist group might use — set off in a large city.

The casualties from such attacks would range from 220,000 to 2,500,000 dead and from 420,000 to 1,100,000 injured, depending on the details of the attack and the prevailing conditions. The discussion in Chapter 3 shows how the time of day, time of year, weather conditions, size of weapon, height of burst, and preparation of the population could all make a great difference in the number of casualties resulting from such an attack.

Case 2.   To examine the effects of a small attack on industrial targets, the book next examines a hypothetical attack limited to 10 SNDVs (strategic nuclear delivery vehicles, the term used in SALT to designate one missile or one bomber) on the other superpower's oil refineries. In "planning" this attack, it was hypothesized that the political leadership instructed the military to inflict maximum damage on energy production using only 10 SNDVs, without any regard for the extent of civilian casualties or other damage. The Soviets were assumed to attack such targets with SS-18 missiles (each carrying 10 multiple independently targetable reentry vehicles, or MIRVs). The United States was assumed to use 7 MIRVed Poseidon missiles and 3 MIRVed Minuteman III missiles.

The calculations detailed in Chapter 5 show that the Soviet attack would destroy 64 percent of U.S. oil refining capacity, while the U.S. attack would destroy 73 percent of Soviet refining capacity. Calculations were also made of "prompt fatalities," including those killed by blast and fallout, assuming no special civil defense measures; they showed about 5 million U.S. deaths and about 1 million Soviet deaths. The results were different for the two countries for several reasons. Soviet oil refining capacity is more concentrated than U.S. oil refining capacity; hence, a small attack can reach more of it. At the same time, Soviet refineries are located further away from residential areas than U.S. refineries. Finally, Soviet warheads are larger than their U.S.

counterparts and will kill people at a greater distance from the target.

One can only speculate about the consequences of such extensive destruction. Drastic changes would be needed in both the U.S. and Soviet economies to cope with the sudden disappearance of the bulk of oil refining capacity. Productivity in virtually every industrial sector would decline. There would have to be strict allocation of the remaining refined petroleum products. Some Soviet factory workers might end up working in the fields to replace tractors for which fuel was unavailable. The United States might have to ban commuting by automobile, forcing suburban residents to choose between moving and long walks to a bus stop.

It is instructive here to observe the differences between the problems that the United States and the Soviet Union would face. Soviet agricultural production, which is barely adequate in peacetime, would probably decline sharply, and production rates would slow even in essential industries. However, the Soviet system is well adapted for allocating scarce resources to high-priority areas, and for keeping everybody employed. The relative wealth and freedom of the United States brings both advantages and disadvantages. While agriculture and essential industry would probably continue, there would be a staggering organizational problem in making use of resources that now depend on petroleum. What would the employees of an automobile factory or a retail establishment on a highway do if there were virtually no gasoline for cars?

Case 3.   To examine the effects of counterforce attacks on civilian populations and economies, the book next examines attacks on ICBM silos and attacks on silos, bomber bases, and missile submarine bases. Such counterforce attacks have been studied extensively by the executive branch of the U.S. government; OTA surveyed a number of these studies in order to determine the range of possible answers. The details of this survey are presented in Chapter 5.

A counterforce attack would result in relatively little direct blast damage to civilians and economic assets; the main damage would come

TABLE 2.   Summary of Effects

Case	Description	Main causes of civilian damage	Immediate deaths	Middle-term effects	Long-term effects
1	Attack on single city: Detroit and Leningrad; 1 weapon or 10 small weapons.	Blast, fire, & loss of infra-structure; fallout is else-where.	200,00-2,000,000	Many deaths from injuries; center of city difficult to rebuild.	Relatively minor.
2	Attack on oil refineries, limited to 10 missiles.	Blast, fire, secondary fires, fallout. Extensive economic problems from loss of refined petroleum.	1,000,000-5,000,000	Many deaths from injuries; great economic hardship for some years; particular problems for Soviet agriculture and for U.S. socioeconomic organization	Cancer deaths in millions only if attack involves surface bursts.
3	Counterforce attack; includes attack only on ICBM silos as a variant.	Some blast damage if bomber and missile sub-marine bases attacked.	1,000,000-20,000,000	Economic impact of deaths; possible large psychological impact.	Cancer deaths and genetic effects in millions; further millions of effects outside attacked countries.
4	Attack on range of military and economic targets using large fraction of existing arsenal.	Blast and fallout; subsequent economic disruption; possible lack of resources to support surviving population or economic recovery. Possible breakdown of social order. Possible incapacitating psychological trauma.	20,000,000-160,000,000	Enormous economic destruction and disruption. If immediate deaths are in low range, more tens of millions may die subsequently because economy is unable to support them. Major question about whether economic viability can be restored—key variables may be those of political and economic organization. Unpredictable psychological effects.	Cancer deaths and genetic damage in the millions; relatively insignificant in attacked areas, but quite significant elsewhere in the world. Possibility of ecological damage.

For each case, the first section describes a Soviet attack on the United States, and the following section a U.S. attack on the Soviet Union.

from radioactive fallout. The uncertain effects of fallout are enormous and depend primarily on the weather and the extent of fallout sheltering. The calculations made by various agencies of the executive branch show a range in "prompt fatalities" (almost entirely deaths from fallout within the first 30 days) from less than 1 to about 11 percent of the U.S. population and from less than 1 to about 5 percent of the Soviet population. These wide variations occur because of differing assumptions about population distribution and shelter.

What can be concluded from these results? First, if the attack involves surface bursts of many very large weapons, if weather conditions are unfavorable, and if no fallout shelters are created beyond those that presently exist, U.S. deaths could reach 20 million after a counterforce attack, and Soviet deaths more than 10 million. The difference is primarily a result of geography; many Soviet strategic forces are so located that fallout from attacks on them would drift into sparsely populated areas or into China. Second, effective fallout sheltering could save many lives under favorable conditions. But even in the best imaginable case, more than a million people would die in either the United States or the Soviet Union from a counterforce attack.

There would be widespread economic damage and disruption as a result of such attacks. Almost all areas could, in principle, be decontaminated within a few months, but the loss of so many people and the interruption of economic life would be staggering blows. An imponderable is the extent of any lasting psychological impacts.

Case 4.   To predict the destruction generally thought to be the culmination of an escalatory process, the book examines the consequences of a very large attack against a full range of military and economic targets. Here, too, recent calculations by the executive branch were used. These calculations generally assume that a Soviet attack on the United States would be a first strike using most of the Soviet arsenal, while U.S. attacks on the Soviet Union would be retaliatory strikes using only those weapons that might survive a Soviet counterforce attack. These calculations are summarized in the last parts of Chapter 5.

Resulting deaths would far exceed any precedent. These calculations show a range of U.S. deaths from 35 to 77 percent (i.e., from 70 to 160 million dead), and Soviet deaths from 20 to 40 percent of the population. Here again the wide range reflects the effects of varying assumptions about population distribution and sheltering, and, to a lesser extent, differences in assumptions about the targeting policy of the attacker. Soviet casualties are smaller than U.S. casualties because a greater fraction of the Soviet population lives in rural areas, and because U.S. weapons (which have lower average yields) produce less fallout than Soviet weapons.

These calculations reflect only deaths during the first 30 days. Additional millions would be injured, and many would eventually die from lack of adequate medical care. In addition, millions of people might starve or freeze during the following winter, but it is impossible to estimate how many. Chapter 6 estimates how many additional millions might eventually die of latent radiation effects.

From the day the survivors emerged from their fallout shelters, a kind of race for survival would begin. One side of the race would be to restore production: production of food, energy, clothing, the means to repair damaged machinery, goods that might be used for trade with countries that had not fought in the war, and even military weapons and supplies. The other side would include the consumption of goods that had survived the attack and the wearing-out of surviving machines. If production rises to the rate of consumption before stocks are exhausted, then viability will have been achieved and economic recovery begun. If not, then each postwar year would see a lower level of economic activity than the year before, and the future of civilization in the nations attacked would be in doubt.

This book cannot predict whether the race for economic viability would be won. The answer would lie in the effectiveness of postwar social and economic organization as much as in the amount of actual physical damage. Would the post-attack economy be based on centralized planning or decentralized decisionmaking? The Charlottesville account of Chapter 1 assumed the former alternative, but one can almost as easily imagine a scenario based on a decentralized organization of society.

Civil defense.   Chapter 4 provides some basic information about civil defense measures. It discusses how they might mitigate the effects of nuclear attack and examines the uncertainties about their effectiveness. There is a lively controversy about the effectiveness of existing Soviet civil defense programs, and another controversy about whether existing U.S. programs ought to be changed. For the purposes of this study, however, the existing civil defense programs, as described in this book, are assumed to be in effect. A full-scale pre-attack evacuation of cities (sometimes called *crisis relocation*) is assumed not to occur. While both the U.S. and the Soviet Governments profess to believe that urban evacuation prior to an attack on cities would save lives, ordering such an evacuation would be a crisis management move that could panic the people in either country and might even increase the risk of a nuclear war actually breaking out.

Long-term effects.   While the immediate damage from the blasts would certainly be long term in the sense that the damage could not be quickly repaired, there would be other effects of nuclear war that might not manifest themselves for some years. Levels of radiation too low (or too slowly absorbed) to cause immediate death or even illness will nevertheless have adverse effects on some fraction of the population receiving (called *static overpressure*) that can crush objects, and high winds (called *dynamic pressure*) that can move them suddenly or knock them down. In general, large buildings are destroyed by the overpressure, while people and objects such as trees and utility poles are destroyed by the wind.

For example, consider the effects of a 1 megaton (Mt) air burst on things 4 miles [6 km] away. The overpressure (generally measured in pounds per square inch, or psi) will be in excess of 5 psi, which will exert a force of more than 180 tons on the wall of a typical two-story house. At the same place, there would be a wind of 160 mph [255

km]. While 5 psi is
wind of 160 mph v
tween people and

The magnitude
with distance fron
earth's surface clc
sion. This magnitu
cated way to the h
level. For any giv
there is an optim
duce the greatest
distance from grc
mum burst heigh
face produces th

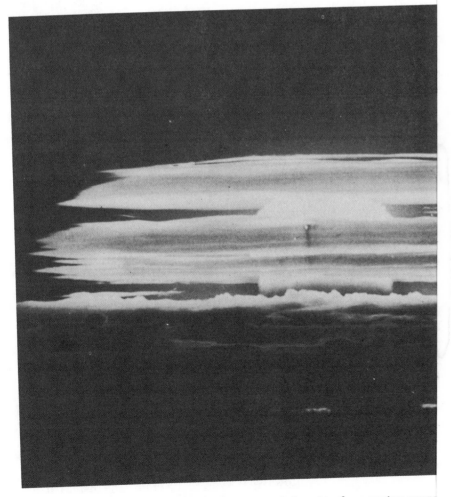

Fireball from an air burst in the megaton energ

The energy of a nuclear explosion can be released by:

- An explosive blast, which is qualitatively similar to the blast from ordinary chemical explosions but has somewhat different effects because it is typically so much larger.
- Direct nuclear radiation.
- Direct thermal radiation, most of which occurs as visible light.
- Pulses of electrical and magnetic energy, called *electromagnetic pulse* (EMP).
- The creation of a variety of radioactive particles, which are thrown up into the air by the force of the blast, and are called radioactive *fallout* when they return to ground.

The distribution of the bomb's energy among these effects depends on its size and on the details of its design, but a general description is possible.

BLAST EFFECTS

Most of the damage to cities from large weapons comes from the explosive blast. The blast drives air away from the site of the explosion, producing sudden changes in air pressure

Thermonuclear ground burst

3

The Effects of Nuclear W

The effects of a nuclear explosion over an urban area wou
somewhat unpredictable. They would vary according t
exact geographical layout of the target area, the materials
construction in the target area, and the weather—especia
ture in the atmosphere. To convey some sense of the actua
explosions, their potential impact is described in two r
Leningrad. To show how these effects vary with the s
effects have been estimated in each city for a variety of w

The descriptions and analysis assume no damage els
which appears unlikely. A surface burst, for example, wo
would cause many casualties elsewhere. However, is
single city allows a clear description of the direct an
nuclear explosions. The result is a kind of tutorial in nu
chapters, which examine the effects of larger attacks, dis
of nuclear fallout and economic and social disruption.

Recently, there has been considerable public interest i
explosion that a terrorist group might set off in an urba
discussed at the end of this chapter.

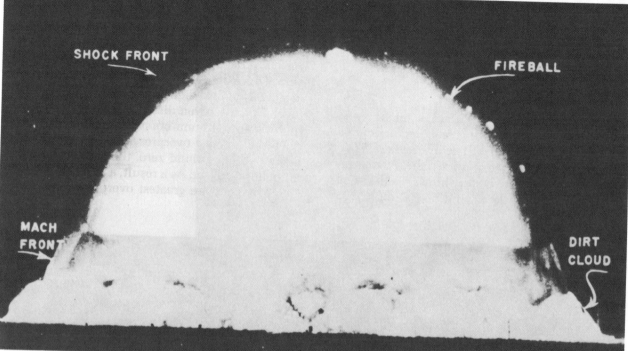

SHOCK FRONT

FIREBALL

MACH FRONT

DIRT CLOUD

The faintly luminous shock front seen just ahead of the fireball soon after breakaway

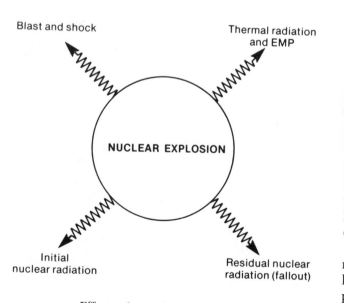

Blast and shock

Thermal radiation and EMP

NUCLEAR EXPLOSION

Initial nuclear radiation

Residual nuclear radiation (fallout)

Effects of a nuclear explosion

close ranges (which is why surface bursts are used to attack very hard, very small targets such as missile silos), but less overpressure than an air burst at somewhat longer ranges. Raising the height of the burst reduces the overpressure directly under the bomb, but widens the area in which a particular smaller overpressure is produced. Thus, an attack on factories with a 1 Mt weapon might use an air burst at an altitude of 8,000 feet [2,400 m], which would maximize the area (about 28 square miles [7,200 hectares]) that would receive 10 psi or more of overpressure. Ranges of overpressure, wind velocity, and blast effects are presented in Table 3.

When a nuclear weapon is detonated on or near the surface of the earth, the blast digs out a large crater. Some of the material removed is deposited on the rim of the crater; the rest is carried up into the air and returns to earth as fallout. An

TABLE 3.   Blast Effects of a 1 Mt Explosion 8,000 ft Above the Earth's Surface

Distance from ground zero		Peak overpressure	Peak wind velocity (mph)	Typical blast effects
(stat. miles)	(kilometers)			
.8	1.3	20 psi	470	Reinforced concrete structures are leveled.
3.0	4.8	10 psi	290	Most factories and commercial buildings are collapsed. Small wood-frame and brick residences destroyed and distributed as debris.
4.4	7.0	5 psi	160	Lightly constructed commercial buildings and typical residences are destroyed; heavier construction is severely damaged.
5.9	9.5	3 psi	95	Walls of typical steel-frame buildings are blown away; severe damage to residences. Winds sufficient to kill people in the open.
11.6	18.6	1 psi	35	Damage to structures; people endangered by flying glass and debris.

explosion that occurs further above the earth's surface than the radius of the fireball does not dig a crater and produces negligible immediate fallout.

For the most part, a nuclear blast kills people by indirect means rather than by direct pressure. While a human body can withstand up to 30 psi of simple overpressure, the winds associated with as little as 2 to 3 psi could be expected to blow people out of typical modern office buildings. Most blast deaths result from the collapse of occupied buildings, from people being blown into objects, or from buildings or smaller objects being blown onto or into people. It is impossible to calculate with any precision how many people would be killed by a given blast; the effects would vary from building to building.

To estimate the number of casualties from any given explosion, it is necessary to make assumptions about the proportion of people who would be killed or injured at any given overpressure. The assumptions used in this chapter are shown in Figure 1; they are relatively conservative. For example, weapons tests suggest that a typical wood-frame house collapses under an overpressure of about 5 psi. People standing in such a house have a 50 percent chance of being killed by

an overpressure of 3.5 psi, but people who are lying down when the blast wave hits have a 50 percent chance of surviving a 7 psi overpressure. Our calculations assume a mean lethal overpressure of 5 to 6 psi for people in residences, meaning that more than half of those whose houses are blown down on top of them will survive. Other studies use a simpler technique: they assume that the number of people who survive in areas receiving more than 5 psi equal the number of people

FIGURE 1.   Vulnerability of Population in Various Overpressure Zones

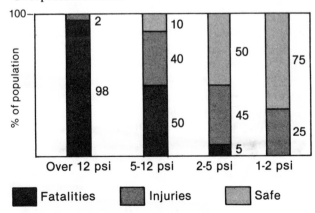

killed in areas receiving less than 5 psi, and hence that fatalities are equal to the number of people inside a 5 psi ring.

DIRECT NUCLEAR RADIATION

Nuclear weapons inflict ionizing radiation on people, animals, and plants in two different ways. *Direct radiation* occurs at the time of the explosion; it can be very intense, but its range is limited. Fallout radiation is received from particles that are made radioactive by the effects of the explosion and are subsequently distributed at varying distances from the site of the blast.

For large nuclear weapons in the megaton category, the range of intense direct radiation is less than the range of lethal blast and thermal radiation effects. But in the case of smaller weapons, direct radiation may be the lethal effect with the greatest range. Direct radiation substantially affected the residents of Hiroshima and Nagasaki.

Human response to ionizing radiation is a subject of great scientific uncertainty and intense controversy. Even small doses of radiation probably do some harm. To understand the effects of nuclear weapons, one must distinguish between short- and long-term effects.

Short-term effects. A radiation dose of 600 rem within a week has a 90 percent chance of causing a fatal illness, with death occurring within a few weeks. (A *rem*, or roentgen-equivalent-man, is a measure of biological damage; a *rad* is a measure of radiation energy absorbed; a *roentgen* is a measure of radiation energy. For our purposes it may be assumed that 100 roentgens produce 100 rads and 100 rem.) The precise relationship of the death rate to the radiation dose is not known in the region between 300 and 600 rem, but it is estimated that a dose of 450 rem within a short time will cause a fatal illness in half the people exposed to it. The other half will get very sick, but will usually recover. A dose of 200 to 450 rem will cause a severe illness from which most people will recover; however, this illness will render people highly susceptible to other diseases or infections. A dose of 50 to 200 rem will cause nausea and lower resistance to other diseases, but medical treatment will not be required. A dose below 50 rem will not cause any short-term effects that the victim will notice, but will nevertheless do long-term damage.

Long-term effects. The principal effects of smaller doses of radiation are long-term and measured statistically. A dose of 50 rem generally produces no short-term effects; however, if a large population is exposed to 50 rems, somewhere between 0.4 and 2.5 percent of them will eventually contract fatal cancer. There will also be serious genetic damage for some fraction of those exposed. Smaller doses will produce less damage. There is a scientific controversy about whether any dose of radiation, however small, is really safe. However, a large nuclear war would expose the survivors, however well sheltered, to levels of radiation far greater than the U.S. Government considers safe in peacetime.

THERMAL RADIATION

Approximately 35 percent of the energy from a nuclear explosion is an intense burst of thermal radiation, or heat. The effects are roughly analogous to the effect of a 2 second flash from an enormous sunlamp. Since the thermal radiation travels at essentially the speed of light, the flash of light and heat precedes the blast wave by several seconds, just as lightning is seen before the thunder is heard.

The visible light will produce *flashblindness* in people who are looking in the direction of the explosion. Flashblindness can last for several minutes, after which recovery is usually total. A 1 Mt explosion could cause flashblindness at distances as great as 13 miles [21 km] on a clear day, or 53 miles [85 km] on a clear night. If the flash is focused through the lens of the eye, a permanent retinal burn will result. At Hiroshima and Nagasaki, there were many cases of flashblindness, but only one case of retinal burn, among the survivors. However, anyone flashblinded while driving a car could easily cause permanent injury or death.

Skin burns result from higher intensities of light and therefore occur closer to the point of explosion. A 1 Mt explosion can cause first-degree burns (equivalent to a bad sunburn) at distances of about 7 miles [11 km], second-degree burns (producing blisters that lead to infection if untreated) at distances of about 6 miles [10 km], and third-degree burns (which destroy skin tissue) at distances of up to 5 miles [8 km]. Third-degree burns over 24 percent of the body, or second-degree burns over 30 percent of the body, will result in serious shock and will probably prove fatal unless prompt, specialized medical care is available. The entire United States has facilities to treat one or two thousand severe burn cases; a single nuclear weapon could produce more than ten thousand.

The distance at which dangerous burns occur depends heavily on weather conditions. Extensive moisture or a high concentration of particles in the air (smog) absorbs thermal radiation. Because thermal radiation behaves like sunlight, objects create shadows behind which the thermal radiation is indirect (reflected) and less intense. Some conditions, such as ice on the ground or low white clouds over clean air, can increase the range of dangerous thermal radiation.

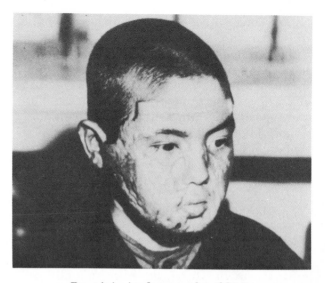

Burn injuries from nuclear blast

FIRES

The thermal radiation from a nuclear explosion can directly ignite kindling materials. In general, kindling materials outside the house, such as dry leaves or newspapers, are not surrounded by enough combustible material to generate a self-sustaining fire. Fires more likely to spread are those caused by thermal radiation passing through windows to ignite beds and overstuffed furniture inside houses. A substantial amount of combustible material must burn vigorously for 10 to 20 minutes before the room, or whole house, becomes inflamed. The blast wave, which arrives after most thermal energy has been expended, will have some extinguishing effect on the fires. However, studies and tests of this effect have been contradictory, so the extent to which blast can be counted on to extinguish fire starts remains uncertain.

Another possible source of fires is blast damage to stoves, water heaters, furnaces, electrical

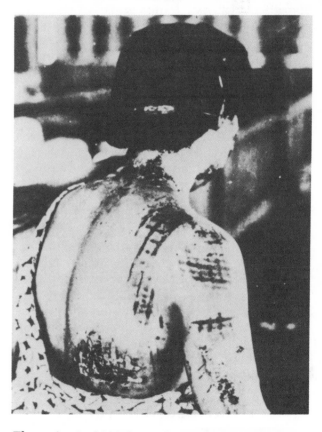

The patient's skin is burned in a pattern corresponding to the dark portions of a kimono worn at the time of the explosion.

circuits, or gas lines — any of which could ignite fires where fuel is plentiful. According to the best estimates, about 10 percent of all buildings would have a serious fire at 5 psi overpressure, while at 2 psi about 2 percent would have serious fires, usually arising from secondary sources such as blast-damaged utilities rather than thermal radiation.

Individual fires, whether caused by thermal radiation or by blast damage to utilities, furnaces, and so on, could coalesce into a massive fire that would consume all structures over a large urban area. This possibility has been studied intensively, but there remains no basis for estimating its probability. Massive fires could be of two kinds: a *firestorm,* in which violent inrushing winds create extremely high temperatures but prevent the fire from spreading radially outwards, and a *conflagration,* in which a fire spreads along a front. Hamburg, Tokyo, and Hiroshima experienced firestorms in World War II; the Great Chicago Fire and the San Francisco Earthquake Fire were conflagrations. A firestorm is likely to kill a high proportion of the people in the area of the fire, through heat and through asphyxiation of those in shelters. A conflagration spreads slowly enough so that people in its path can escape, although a conflagration caused by a nuclear attack might take a heavy toll of those too injured to walk. Some believe that firestorms in U.S. or Soviet cities are unlikely because the density of flammable materials *(fuel loading)* is too low — the ignition of a firestorm is thought to require a fuel loading of at least 8 lb/ft^2 (Hamburg had 32), compared to fuel loading of 2 lb/ft^2 in a typical U.S. suburb and 5 lb/ft^2 in a neighborhood of two-story brick rowhouses. The likelihood of a conflagration depends on the geography of the area, the speed and direction of the wind, and details of building construction. Another variable is whether people and equipment are available to fight fires before they can coalesce and spread.

ELECTROMAGNETIC PULSE

Electromagnetic pulse (EMP) is an electromagnetic wave, similar to radio waves, that occurs when the nuclear gamma radiation is absorbed in the air or ground. It differs from normal radio waves in two important ways. First, it creates much higher electric field strengths. Whereas a radio signal might produce a thousandth of a volt or less in a receiving antenna, an electromagnetic pulse can produce *thousands* of volts. Secondly, it is a single pulse of energy that disappears completely in a small fraction of a second. In this sense, it is rather similar to the electrical signal from lightning, but the rise in voltage is typically a hundred times faster. Most equipment designed to protect electrical facilities from lightning works too slowly to be effective against EMP.

A nuclear weapon burst on the surface will typically produce an EMP of tens of thousands of volts per meter (of antenna) at short distances (the 10 psi range) and thousands of volts per meter at longer distances (1 psi range). Air bursts produce weaker EMP, but high-altitude bursts (above 19 miles [30 km]) produce very strong EMP, with ranges of hundreds or thousands of miles. An attacker might first detonate a few weapons at such altitudes in an effort to destroy or damage the communications and electric power systems of the victim.

There is no evidence that EMP is a physical threat to people. However, electrical or electronic systems, particularly those connected to long wires such as powerlines or antennas, can undergo either of two kinds of damage. First, there can be actual physical damage to an electrical component such as shorting of a capacitor or burnout of a transistor, which would require replacement or repair before the equipment could again be used. Radio stations are especially vulnerable to this type of damage. Second, there can be a temporary operational upset, frequently requiring some effort to restore operation. For example, instabilities induced in power grids can cause the entire system to shut itself down, upsetting computers that must be started again. In general, portable radio transmitters and receivers with relatively short antennas are not very susceptible to EMP. The vulnerability of the telephone system to EMP has not yet been reliably determined.

RADIOACTIVE FALLOUT

While any nuclear explosion in the atmosphere produces some fallout, the fallout is far greater if the burst is on the surface, or low enough for the fireball to touch the ground. As Chapter 6 shows in some detail, the fallout from air bursts alone poses long-term health hazards, but they are trivial compared with the other consequences of a nuclear attack. The most significant hazards come from particles scooped up from the ground and irradiated by the nuclear explosion.

The radioactive particles that rise only a short distance (those in the "stem" of the familiar mushroom cloud) will fall back to earth within a matter of minutes, landing close to the center of the explosion. Such particles are unlikely to cause many deaths, because they will fall in areas where most people have already been killed. However, the intense radioactivity will complicate efforts at rescue or eventual reconstruction.

The radioactive particles that rise higher will be carried some distance by the wind before returning to earth. Thus, the area and intensity of the fallout is strongly influenced by local weather conditions. Much of the material is simply blown downwind in a long plume. The map in Figure 2 illustrates the fallout pattern, or "plume," expected from a 1 Mt surface burst in Detroit if winds were blowing toward Canada. The illustrated plume was calculated by assuming that the winds were blowing at a uniform speed of 15 mph [24 kmh] over the entire region. The plume would be longer and thinner if the winds were more intense, and shorter and somewhat broader if the winds were slower. If the winds were from a different direction, the plume would cover a different area. For example, a wind from the northwest would deposit enough fallout on Cleveland (see Figure 3) to inflict acute radiation sickness on those who did not evacuate or use effective fallout shelters. Thus, wind direction can make an enormous difference.

Rainfall can also have a significant influence on the ways in which radiation from smaller weapons is deposited, since rain will carry contaminated particles to the ground. Areas receiving such contaminated rainfall would become "hot spots," with greater radiation intensity than their surroundings. If radiation intensity from fallout was great enough to pose an immediate threat to health, fallout would generally be visible as a thin layer of dust.

The amount of radiation produced by fallout materials decreases with time as the radioactive materials "decay." Each material decays at a different rate. Materials that decay rapidly give off intense radiation for a short period of time while long-lived materials radiate less intensely but for longer periods. Immediately after the fallout is deposited in regions surrounding the blast site, radiation intensities are very high as the short-lived materials rapidly decay. This intense radiation decreases relatively quickly. The intensity will have fallen by a factor of 10 after 7 hours, a factor of 100 after 49 hours and a factor of 1,000 after 2 weeks. The areas in the plumes illustrated in Figures 2 and 3 would become "safe" (by peacetime standards) in 2 to 3 years for the outer ellipse, and in 10 years or so for the inner ellipse.

Some radioactive particles are thrust into the stratosphere and may not return to earth for years. In this case only the particularly long-lived particles pose a threat, and they are dispersed around the world over a range of latitudes. Some fallout from U.S. and Soviet weapons tests in the 1950s and early 1960s can still be detected. There are also some particles in the immediate fallout (notably Strontium 90 and Cesium 137) that remain radioactive for years. Chapter 6 discusses some of the likely hazards from these long-lived particles.

The biological effects of fallout radiation are substantially the same as those from direct radiation, discussed above. People exposed to enough fallout radiation will die, and those exposed to lesser amounts may become ill. Chapter 4 discusses the theory of fallout sheltering, and Chapter 5 some of the practical difficulties of escaping fallout from a large counterforce attack.

There has been recent public interest in the question of the consequences of a nuclear weapon destroying a nuclear powerplant. The

FIGURE 2. Main Fallout Pattern—Uniform 15 mph Southwest Wind. 1 Mt surface burst on Detroit; contours for seven day accumulated dose without shielding of 3,000, 900, 300 and 90 rem.

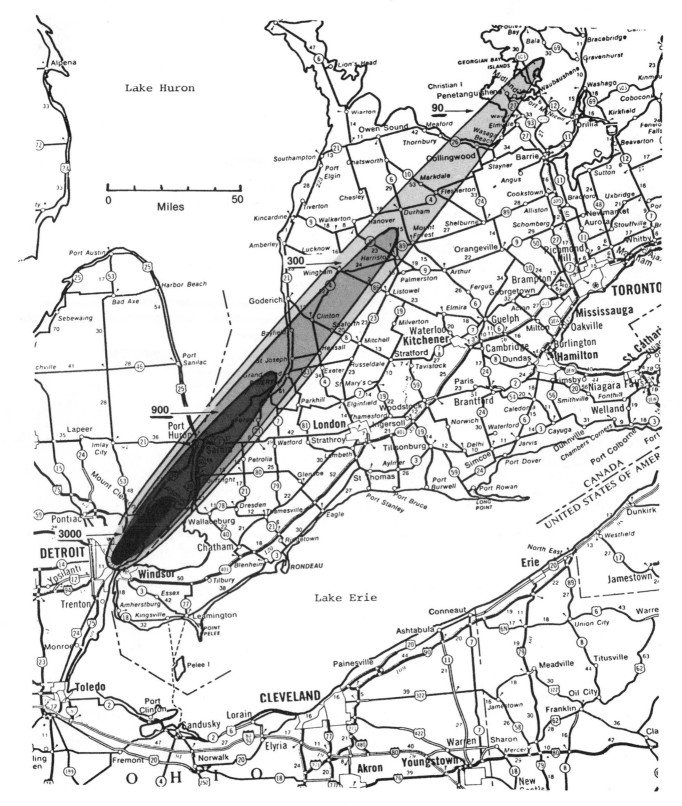

FIGURE 3. Main Fallout Pattern—Uniform 15 mph Northwest Wind. 1 Mt surface burst on Detroit; contours for seven day accumulated dose without shielding of 3,000, 900, 300, and 90 rem.

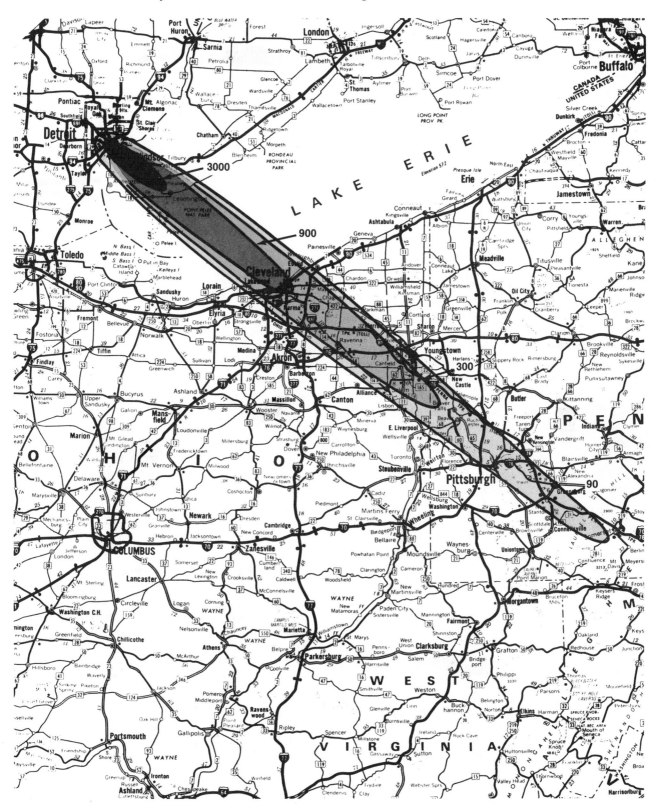

core of a power reactor contains large quantities of radioactive material, which tends to decay more slowly (and hence less intensely) than the fallout particles from a nuclear weapon explosion. Consequently, fallout from a destroyed nuclear reactor (whose destruction would, incidently, require a high-accuracy surface burst) would not be much more intense (during the first day) or widespread than "ordinary" fallout, but would stay radioactive for a considerably longer time. Areas receiving such fallout would have to be evacuated or decontaminated; otherwise, survivors would have to stay in shelters for months.

COMBINED INJURIES

So far the discussion of each major effect of a nuclear explosion has explained how this effect *in isolation* causes deaths and injuries. It is customary to calculate the casualties accompanying a hypothetical nuclear explosion as follows: for any given range, the effect most likely to kill people is selected and its consequences calculated, while the other effects are ignored. Although combined injuries are obviously possible, there are no generally accepted ways of calculating their probability. What information does exist seems to suggest that calculations of single effects are accurate enough for immediate deaths, but that deaths occurring some time after the explosion may well be due to combined causes. Some of the obvious possibilities are:

- nuclear radiation combined with thermal radiation;
- nuclear radiation combined with mechanical injuries;
- thermal radiation combined with mechanical injuries.

In the first instance, severe burns place considerable stress on the blood system, and often cause anemia. Experiments with laboratory animals show that exposure of a burn victim to more than 100 rems will impair the blood's ability to support recovery from thermal burns. Hence a suble-

thal radiation dose could make it impossible to recover from a burn that, without the radiation, would not cause death.

Mechanical injuries—the indirect results of blast—take many forms. Flying glass and wood will cause puncture wounds. Winds may blow people into obstructions, causing broken bones, concussions, and internal injuries. Persons caught in a collapsing building can suffer many similar mechanical injuries. There is evidence that all of these types of injuries are more serious if the person has been exposed to 300 rems, particularly if treatment is delayed. Blood damage will clearly make a victim more susceptible to blood loss and infection. This has been confirmed in laboratory animals in which a borderline lethal radiation dose was followed a week later by a blast overpressure that alone would have produced a low level of prompt deaths. The number of prompt and delayed deaths both increased over what would be expected from the single effect alone.

Mechanical injuries should be prevalent at about the distance from a nuclear explosion that produces sublethal burns, and synergy between the two effects could be fatal. In general, synergistic effects are most likely to cause death when each of the injuries alone is quite severe. Because the uncertainties of nuclear effects are compounded when one tries to estimate the likelihood of two or more serious but individually non-fatal injuries, there really is no way to estimate the number of fatalities.

A further dimension of the problem is the possible synergy between injuries and environmental damage. For example, poor sanitation due to the loss of electrical power and water pressure can clearly compound the effects of any serious injury. Also, an injury could so immobilize the victim that he or she would be unable to escape from a fire.

DETROIT

Detroit is a representative industrial city large enough to warrant the use of very large weapons.

Skyline of Detroit

It has a metropolitan population of about 4.3 million and is a major transportation and industrial center.

In assessing and describing the damage from nuclear explosions, several assumptions were made that may not be realistic, but which helped make a clear presentation of the range of possible effects:

- There is no warning; the population has not evacuated or sought shelter, two measures that could reduce casualties.

- Detonations take place at night when most people are at their residences. According to available census data, people are near their residences more than half the time.

- There is clear weather, with visibility of 10 miles [16 km].

- Air bursts are at an altitude that maximizes the area of 30 psi or more overpressure. A higher burst would increase the range of 5 psi overpressure (i.e., destruction of all residences) by up to 10 percent, but decrease the damage to very hard structures near ground zero.

• No other cities are attacked, so one can analyze the extent of outside help that would be required, were it available.

A 1 MT SURFACE BURST ON DETROIT

The metropolitan area of Detroit is shown in Figure 4, with Windsor, Canada, across the river to the southeast and Lake St. Clair directly east. The detonation occurs at the intersection of Interstate Highways I-75 and I-94, approximately at the civic center and about 3 miles [5 km] from the Detroit-Windsor tunnel entrance. Circles indicate the 12, 5, 2, and 1 psi overpressure limits.

Physical Damage

The 1 Mt explosion on the surface leaves a crater about 1,000 feet [300 m] in diameter and 200 feet [61 m] deep, surrounded by a rim of highly radioactive soil about twice this diameter. Out to a distance of 0.6 miles [1 km] from the center, nothing recognizable remains, with the exception of some massive concrete bridge abutments and building foundations. At 0.6 miles some heavily damaged highway bridge sections remain, but there is little else until 1.3 miles [2.1 km], where a few strongly constructed buildings with poured reinforced concrete walls survive. But the interiors are totally destroyed by the blast wave that enters the window openings. A distance of 1.7 miles [2.7 km] (12 psi ring) is the closest range where a significant number of structures remain.

Of the 70,000 people in this area during nonworking hours, there are virtually no survivors. (See Table 4.) Fatalities during working hours in this business district would have undoubtedly been much higher. The estimated daytime population of the downtown area is something over 200,000 in contrast to the census data of about 15,000. If the attack occurred during daytime, the fatalities would increase by 130,000 and injuries by 45,000 over the estimates in Table 4. There would be some reduction in casualties in outlying residential areas, where the daytime population would be lower.

In the ring between the 1.7 and the 2.7 mile (5 psi) circles, typical commercial and residential multistory buildings have their walls completely blown out, but increasingly at the greater distances the skeletal structures remain standing.

Individual residences in this ring are totally destroyed, with only foundations and basements remaining, and the debris are uniformly distributed over the area. Heavy industrial plants are destroyed in the inner part of the ring, but some industry remains functional towards the outer edge. The depth of the debris that clutters the streets depends on both the height of buildings and how closely together they are spaced. Typical depths range from tens of feet in the downtown area where buildings are 10 to 20 stories high, to several inches where buildings are lower and streets broader in the area to the west and north. In this ring, blast damage alone destroys all automobiles, while some heavier commercial vehicles (firetrucks and repair vehicles) survive near the outer edges. However, few vehicles are sufficiently protected from debris to remain useful. The parking lots of both Cobb Field and Tiger Stadium contain nothing driveable.

In this same ring, which contains a nighttime population of about 250,000, about half are killed, with most of the remainder injured. Most deaths occur from collapsing buildings. Although many fires are started, only a small percentage of the buildings continue to burn after the blast wave passes. The mechanics of fire spread in a heavily damaged and debris-strewn area are not well understood. However, fire spread probably would be slow and there would be no firestorm. For unprotected people, direct nuclear radiation is lethal out to about 1.7 miles [2.7 km], but insignificant in its immediate effects (50 rems) at 2.0 miles [3.2 km]. Since few people inside a 2 mile ring survive the blast, and they are likely to be in strong buildings, additional fatalities and injuries from direct nuclear radiation should be small compared to other uncertainties.

The number of casualties from thermal burns depends on the time of day, season, and atmospheric visibility. Modest variations in these factors produce huge changes in vulnerability to burns. For example, on a winter night less than 1 percent of the population would be exposed to

FIGURE 4. Detroit — 1 Mt Surface Burst

12 psi

5 psi

2 psi

1 psi

0   2   4   6   8   10
Miles

TABLE 4.   Casualty Estimates (in thousands)

Region (mi)	Area (mi²)	Population	Fatalities	Injuries	Uninjured
0-1.7	9.1	70	70	0	0
1.7-2.7	13.8	250	130	100	20
2.7-4.7	46.5	400	20	180	200
4.7-7.4	102.6	600	0	150	450

TABLE 5.   Burn Casualty Estimates (1 Mt on Detroit)

Distance from blast (mi)	Survivors of blast effects	Fatalities (eventual)		Injuries	
		2-mile visibility	10-mile visibility	2-mile visibility	10-mile visibility
(1 percent of population exposed to line of sight from fireball)					
0-1.7	0	0	0	0	0
1.7-2.7	120,000	1,200	1,200	0	0
2.7-4.7	380,000	0	3,800	500	0
4.7-7.4	600,000	0	2,600	0	3,000
Total (rounded) . .		1,000	8,000	500	3,000
(25 percent of population exposed to line of sight from fireball)					
0-1.7	0	0	0	0	0
1.7-2.7	120,000	30,000	30,000	0	0
2.7-4.7	380,000	0	95,000	11,000	0
4.7-7.4	600,000	0	66,000	0	75,000
Total (rounded) . .		30,000	190,000	11,000	75,000

These calculations arbitrarily assume that exposure to more than 6.7 cal/cm² produces eventual death, and exposure to more than 3.4 cal/cm² produces a significant injury, requiring specialized medical treatment.

direct thermal radiation, while on a clear summer weekend afternoon more than 25 percent might be exposed (that is, have no structure between the fireball and the person). When visibility is 10 miles [16 km], a 1 Mt explosion produces second-degree burns at a distance of 6 miles [10 km], while under circumstances when visibility is 2 miles [3 km], the range of second-degree burns is only 2.7 miles [4.3 km]. This variation could cause deaths from thermal radiation to vary between 1,000 and 190,000, and injuries to vary between 500 and 75,000 (see Table 5).

In the ring from 2.7 to 4.7 miles [4.4 to 7.6 km] (2 psi), large buildings have lost windows, frames, and interior partitions. In those with light-walled construction, most of the contents of upper floors have been blown out into the streets. Load-bearing walls in buildings at the University of Detroit are severely cracked. Low residential

buildings are totally destroyed or severely damaged. Casualties are estimated to be about 50 percent in this region — mostly injuries. There is substantial debris in the streets, but a significant number of cars and trucks remain operable. In this ring, damage to heavy industrial plants, such as the Cadillac plant, is severe, and most planes and hangars at the Detroit City Airport have been destroyed.

In this ring only 5 percent of the population of about 400,000 has been killed, but nearly half are injured (Table 4). This is the region of the most severe fire hazard, since fire ignition and spread is more likely in partly damaged buildings than in completely flattened areas. Perhaps 5 percent of the buildings are initially ignited, with fire spread to adjoining buildings very likely if their separation is less than 50 feet [15 m]. Fires continue to spread for at least 24 hours, ultimately

Blast damage to brick house (5 psi overpressure)

destroying about half the buildings. However, these estimates are extremely uncertain because they are based on poor data and unknown weather conditions. They also assume that the uninjured half of the population makes no effective effort to prevent the ignition or spread of fires.

As Table 5 shows, there are between 4,000 and 95,000 additional deaths from thermal radiation in this band, assuming a visibility of 10 miles [16 km]. A 2 mile [3 km] visibility, however, would only produce between 500 and 11,000 severely injured, but many of these would subsequently die because of inadequate medical treatment.

In the outermost band (4.7 to 7.4 miles [7.6 to 11.9 km]) there is only light damage to commercial structures and moderate damage to residences. Casualties are estimated at 25 percent injured and only an insignificant number killed (Table 4). Under the range of conditions displayed in Table 5, there are an additional 3,000 to 75,000 burn injuries requiring specialized medical care. Fire ignitions are comparatively rare (limited to such kindling material as newspaper and dry leaves) and easily controlled by the survivors.

Whether fallout comes from the stem or the cap of the mushroom is a major concern in the general vicinity of the detonation because of the time element and its effect on general emergency operations. Fallout from the stem starts building after about 10 minutes, and during the first hour after detonation it represents the primary radiation threat to emergency crews. The affected area has a radius of about 6.5 miles [10.5 km] (as indicated by the dashed curve on Figure 4) with a hot spot at a downwind distance that depends on the wind velocity. If a 15 mph wind from the southwest is assumed, people with no fallout protection at all in an area of about 1 mi^2 [260 hectares]—the solid ellipse shown—would receive an average exposure of 300 rems in the first hour. The larger toned ellipse shows the area of 150 rems exposure in the first hour. But the important feature of short-term (up to 1 hour) fallout is the relatively small area covered by life-threatening radiation levels compared to the area covered by blast damage.

Starting about an hour after detonation the main fallout from the cloud itself starts to arrive, and some of it adds to the already-deposited local stem fallout, but the bulk is distributed in an elongated downward ellipse. The two fallout patterns shown in Figures 2 and 3 differ only in the direction of the wind. The contours are marked with the number of rems received in the week following the arrival of the cloud fallout, again assuming no fallout protection whatever. Realistic patterns, which would reflect wind shear, a wider crosswind distribution, and other atmospheric variables, would be far more complex than this illustration.

Rescue and Recovery

The half-million injured in the blast present a medical task of incredible magnitude.[1] Those parts of Wayne, Macomb, and Oakland counties shown on the map have 63 hospitals containing about 18,000 beds. However, 55 percent of these beds are inside the 5 psi ring and have thus been destroyed. Another 15 percent in the 2 to 5 psi band have been severely damaged, leaving 5,000 beds remaining outside the region of significant damage. Since this is only 1 percent of the number of injured, the Detroit area hospitals are incapable of providing significant medical assistance. In the first few days, transport of injured out of the damaged area is severely hampered by debris clogging the streets. In general, only the nonprofessional assistance of nearby survivors can help hold down the large number of subsequent deaths. Even as transportation for the injured out of the area becomes available in subsequent days, the total medical facilities of the United States are severely overburdened; in 1977 there were only 1,407,000 hospital beds in the whole United States. Burn victims number in the tens of thousands, but in 1977 there were only 85 specialized burn centers, with probably 1,000 to 2,000 beds, in the entire United States.

There is a total loss of all utilities in areas with significant physical damage to the basic structure of buildings. The collapse of buildings and the toppling of trees and utility poles, along with the injection of tens of thousands of volts from EMP into wires, causes the immediate loss of power in a major sector of the total U.S. power grid. Main electrical powerplants (near Grosse Point Park to the east and Zug Island to the south) are both in the 1 psi ring and suffer only superficial damage. Within a day the major area grid is restored, bringing power back to facilities located outside the 1 psi ring. Large numbers of powerline workers and their equipment brought in from the surrounding states are able to gradually restore service to surviving structures in the 1 to 2 psi ring over a period of days.

The water distribution system is mostly intact since, with the exception of one booster pumping station at 2 psi (which suffers only minor damage), its facilities are outside the damaged area. However, the loss of electric power to the pumps and the breaking of many service connections to destroyed buildings immediately causes the loss of all water pressure. Service to the whole area can be restored only when the regional power grid is restored, and to the areas of light and intermediate damage only as valves to broken pipes can be located and shut off over a period of days. There is only sporadic damage to buried mains in the 2 to 5 psi region, but such damage occurs with increasing frequency in the 5 to 12 psi region. Damaged sections near the explosion center will have to be closed off.

The gas distribution system receives similar damage: loss of pressure from numerous broken service connections and some broken mains, particularly in the 5 to 12 psi ring. There are also numerous fires. Service is slowly restored as utility repairmen and service equipment are brought in from surrounding areas.

Rescue and recovery operations heavily depend on the reestablishment of transportation consisting of private cars, buses, and commercial trucks that use a radial interstate system and a conventional urban grid. Since bridges and overpasses are surprisingly immune to blast effects, those interstate highways and broad urban streets without significant structures nearby survive as far in as the 12 psi ring and can be quickly restored for clearing away minor amounts of debris. However, most urban streets are cluttered with varying quantities of debris, starting with tree limbs and other minor obstacles at 1 psi, and in-

creasing in density up to the 12 psi ring, where all buildings, trees, and cars are smashed and quite uniformly redistributed over the area. It could take weeks or months to remove the debris and restore road transportation in the area.

The Detroit city airport, located in the middle of the 2 to 5 psi ring, has virtually all of its aircraft and facilities destroyed. Usually runways can be quickly restored to use following minor debris removal, but in this particular example with a southwest wind, the airport is the center of the fallout hot spot from the dust column as well as the intensive fallout from the cloud. Thus, cleanup efforts to restore flight operations can not commence for 2 weeks at the earliest, with the workers involved in the cleanup receiving 100 rems accumulated during the third week. The Detroit Metropolitan Wayne County Airport and the Willow Run Airport are far outside the blast effects area and become available as soon as the regional power grid electric service is restored.

The main train station, near the Detroit-Windsor highway tunnel, suffers major damage (5 psi), but since few people commute to the downtown area by train, its loss is not a major factor in the overall paralysis of transportation. The surrounding industry depends heavily on rail transportation, but rail equipment and lines usually survive wherever the facilities they support survive.

Most gasoline fuel oil tanks are located beyond Dearborn and Lincoln Park and, at 16 miles [26 Km] from the detonation, have suffered no damage. Arrival of fuel is not impeded, but its distribution is totally dependent on cleanup of streets and highways.

The civil defense control center, located just beyond the Highland Park area in the 1 to 2 psi ring, is able to function without impairment. Commercial communications systems (television and base radio transmitters) are inoperable both from the loss of commercial power in the area and, for those facilities in the blast area, from EMP. Those not blast damaged can be restored in several days. In the meantime, mobile radio systems provide the primary means of communicating with heavily damaged areas. The telephone system remains largely functional in those areas where the lines have survived structural damage in collapsing buildings, or street damage in areas where they are not buried.

Radioactive Fallout

The extent and location of radioactive fallout depends on weather conditions, especially the speed and direction of the wind. A uniform wind velocity of 15 mph would distribute fallout over sparsely populated farming areas in Canada if the wind is from the southwest, or over Cleveland and Youngstown, Ohio, and Pittsburgh if the wind is from the northwest (see Figures 2 and 3). These fallout patterns are idealized; such neat ellipses would occur in reality only with an absolutely constant wind and no rain.

No effort was made to estimate the deaths, injuries, or economic losses that might result from such fallout patterns. However, the possibilities are instructive. The onset of fallout depends on wind velocity and distance from the explosion and is most dangerous during the first few days. In the case of an attack on a single city (using a surface burst), people living downwind would probably evacuate. Those who neither evacuated nor found adequate fallout shelters would be subjected to dangerous levels of radiation. People in the inner contour (see Figures 2 and 3) would receive a fatal dose within the first week. People in the next contour out would contract severe radiation sickness if they stayed indoors and would probably receive a fatal dose if they spent much time outdoors. People in the next contour out would contract generally nonfatal radiation sickness, with increased hazards of deaths from other diseases. People in the outer contour would suffer few visible effects, but their life expectancy would drop as a result of an increased risk of eventual cancer.

As time passes, the continuing decay of fallout radiation could be accelerated by decontamination. Some decontamination takes place naturally, as rain washes radioactive particles away, and as they are leached into the soil — a process that attenuates radiation. Specific measures can also speed decontamination. Presumably, evacuees would not return to a contaminated area un-

til the effects of time and decontamination made it safe.

If no significant decontamination takes place, areas receiving fallout will become safe only when the radioactive particles have decayed to safe levels. Decay to a level of 500 millirems per year requires 8 to 10 years for the inner contour (3,000 roentgens in the first week), 6 years or so for the next contour (900 roentgens), 3 to 4 years for the next contour (300 roentgens), and about 3 years for the outer contour (90 roentgens). Natural processes could concentrate some radioactive particles, and those that entered the food chain could pose an additional hazard.

Summary

Doubtless there are many uncertainties in the assumptions underlying this description of the results of a 1 Mt surface burst in Detroit. Nevertheless, several salient features stand out:

- seventy square miles of property destruction;
- a quarter million fatalities, plus half a million injuries;
- additional damage from widespread fires.

Casualties could have been greatly reduced by an alert and informed population. But rescue and recovery operations must be organized and heavily supported from outside the area.

A 1 MT AIR BURST ON DETROIT

For comparison, the same 1 Mt nuclear weapon was assumed to have been air burst at an altitude of 6,000 feet [1.8 km] over the same intersection as used in the preceding example. This altitude maximizes the size of the 30 psi circle, but the radius of the 5 psi circle that results is only 10 percent smaller than the largest possible with this 1 Mt weapon. There are several significant differences from the ground burst case:

- The rings of pressure damage are larger.

FIGURE 5.   Detroit — 1 Mt Air Burst

FIGURE 6.   Casualties — Detroit and Leningrad

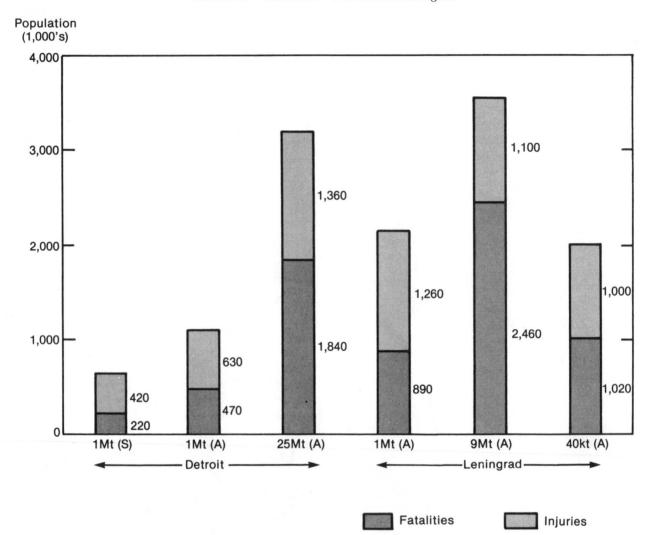

- The range of thermal burns and fire starts also increases.
- There is no significant fallout.
- There is no crater.
- The strongest structures may partly survive even directly under the blast.

Figure 5 shows the corresponding pressure circles; Figure 6 (second column) illustrates that the number of fatalities nearly doubles, and the number of injured greatly increases. Almost half a million deaths and over a million total casualties occur within the first hour after detonation. At the same time, damage to major industrial facilities becomes significant, with the Chrysler plant in the middle of the 2 to 5 psi band, and the Ford River Rouge plant in the 1 to 2 psi band.

A 25 MT AIR BURST ON DETROIT

The 25 Mt case assumes a burst altitude of 17,500 feet [5.3 km] over the same intersection. Figure 7 shows the 12, 5, and 2 psi rings, but the 1 psi ring at 30.4 miles [48.9 km] is completely off

FIGURE 7. Detroit — 25 Mt Air Burst

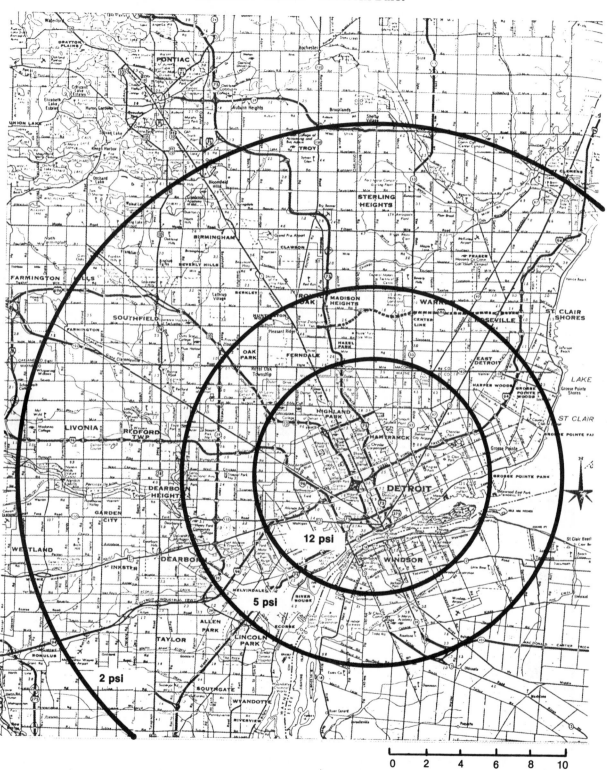

FIGURE 8.   Leningrad — Commercial and Residential Sections

FIGURE 9.   Leningrad — Populated Areas

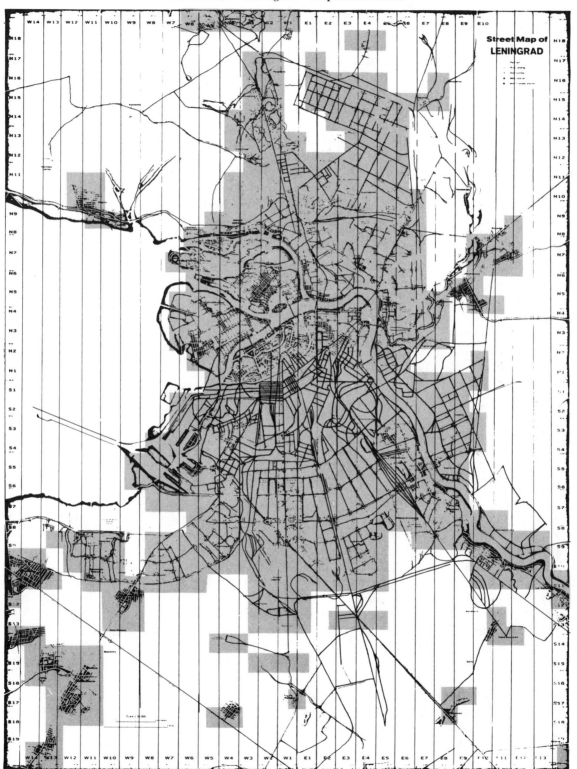

the map. Damage and casualties would increase even further if the detonation point were moved about 5 miles [8 km] to the northwest. But even without this shift, the whole metropolitan area is heavily damaged by the explosive power of this huge weapon. The casualties are shown in Figure 6 (column 3).

There are stark contrasts to the 1 Mt surface burst. Only 1.1 million survivors are available to assist (or bury) the much more numerous casualties — 3.2 million. Contrast this outcome with that of the 1 Mt surface burst, in which 3.7 million survivors were potentially available to assist 640,000 casualties. There is virtually no habitable housing left in the area. Essentially all heavy industry has been totally destroyed. Rescue operations have to be totally supported from outside the Detroit area, with evacuation of the 1.2 million survivors the only feasible course. Recovery and rebuilding will be a long-term, problematical issue.

LENINGRAD

Leningrad is a major industrial and transportation center built on a low-lying delta where the Neva River enters the Gulf of Finland. The older part of the city is built on the delta itself, with the newer residential sections leapfrogging industrial sections, primarily to the south and southwest (Figure 8). The residential and commercial (but not industrial) areas are shown on the map.

The major difference in housing between Leningrad and Detroit is that Leningrad suburbs contain very few single-family residences. In the older part of Leningrad, the buildings have masonry load-bearing walls and wooden interior construction and are typically six to eight stories, reflecting the early code that only church spires could be higher than the Tsar's Winter Palace. The post-World War II housing construction consists of 10- to 12-story apartments with steel frames and precast concrete walls. The buildings are comfortably spaced on wide thoroughfares in open parklike settings.

Because actual population density data for Leningrad was unavailable, simplifying demographic assumptions have been used. The assumed populated areas are shown in Figure 9, broken down into 1 km [0.6-mile] squares. The total area of Leningrad is 500 km^2 [193 mi^2]. Since the shaded squares cover 427 km^2 [165 mi^2], it was assumed that the remaining areas are relatively uninhabited at night. It has also been assumed that in these inhabited areas the population density is uniform at 10,000 people per square kilometer. Finally, the assumptions made for Detroit (see page 49) were also made for nuclear blasts occurring over Leningrad.

1 MT AND 9 MT AIR BURSTS ON LENINGRAD

The Leningrad apartments are likely to have their walls blown out, and the people swept out (at about 5 psi) even though the remaining steel skeleton will withstand much higher pressures. Thus, although the type of construction is totally different from Detroit, the damage levels are so similar that the same relationship between overpressure and casualties occurs (Figure 1).

The 1 Mt and 9 Mt air burst pressure rings are shown in Figures 10 and 11. Note that in the 9 Mt case the 1 psi ring falls completely off the map, as was the case for the 25 Mt warhead on Detroit. Calculated casualties are illustrated in Figure 6 (columns 4 and 5). They are about double those of Detroit for the comparable 1 Mt case, mainly because of the higher average population density. In the 1 Mt explosion, there are over 2 million casualties, with 890,000 deaths. In the 9 Mt case, there are over 3.5 million casualties (in a total population of approximately 4.3 million), leaving less than a million people uninjured. Like Detroit in the 25 Mt explosion, rescue operations must come entirely from outside the city of Leningrad.

There are other contrasts between the two cities; in Leningrad:

- People live near their work. In general, there is no daily cross-city movement.

- Buildings (except in the old part of the city) are unlikely to burn.
- Apartment building spacing is so great that it makes fire spread unlikely, even though a few buildings would burn down.
- There will be much debris preventing access to damaged areas.
- Transportation is by rail to the outlying areas, and by an excellent metro system within the city.
- There is only one television station — in the middle of the city — so mass communications would be interrupted until other broadcasting equipment was brought in and set up.

TEN 40 KT AIR BURSTS ON LENINGRAD

Another possible attack scenario is the delivery of ten small, 40 kt warheads in a pattern selected to maximize the physical damage to the city. A possible selection of burst points, set to have the 5 psi circles touching, is shown in Figure 12. It is assumed that this precise pattern can be achieved in an actual attack. Errors arising from neglecting the overlap of the 2 to 5 psi bands will be negligible compared to uncertainties in population distribution and structural design. Casualty estimates are shown in the righthand column of Figure 6. There are an estimated 2 million casualties, with 1 million deaths. Note that fatalities are only slightly greater than in the 1 Mt case. However, the number of injured is considerably smaller because injuries primarily occur in the 2 to 5 psi band, which is much smaller for the 40 kt pattern than for the single 1 Mt case.

A TERRORIST WEAPON AT GROUND LEVEL

Another nuclear weapon of recent concern is one constructed by terrorists and detonated in a major city.[2] A terrorist group using stolen or diverted fission material and having general technical competence but lacking direct weapon de-

sign experience could probably build a weapon of up to several kilotons. This weapon would be large and heavy, certainly not the often imagined "suitcase bomb." Thus, it is likely to be transported in a van or small truck, with threatened detonation either in the street or the parking garage of a building.

Because of the detonation location and yield of this weapon, its effects will be much less devastating than those of high-yield, strategic weapons. The range and magnitude of all the nuclear effects will be greatly reduced by the low yields. In addition, the relative range of lethal effects will be different. At high yields, blast and thermal burn reach out to greater distances than does direct nuclear radiation. At 1 kt the reverse is true; for example, 5 psi overpressure occurs at 1,450 feet [442 m], while 600 rems of radiation extends to 2,650 feet [808 m]. For the 1 Mt surface burst, 5 psi occurred at 2.7 miles and 600 rems at 1.7 miles.

In addition to these differences in range, the highly built-up urban structure in which the weapon is placed will significantly modify the resulting nuclear environment. The blast effects of a small weapon will probably be severely influenced by nearby structures. For example, suppose a device is detonated in a van parked alongside a 1,000 foot high building in the middle of a block in an urban complex of rather closely spaced streets in one direction and more broadly spaced avenues in the other direction. Whereas the 2.5 psi ring would have a radius of 2,100 feet [640 m] detonated on a smooth surface, this blast wave will extend 2,800 feet [850 m] directly down the street, but only 1,500 feet [450 m] in a random direction angling through the built-up blocks. These calculations have been made by using many approximate factors that, if more accurately represented, would probably lead to an even greater reduction in range.

Other weapons effects will be similarly modified from those predicted on the basis of a relatively open target area. In the case of initial nuclear radiation, a lethal 600 rem would normally extend to 2,650 feet [808 m]. But because of the great absorption of this radiation as it passes through the multiple walls of the several build-

FIGURE 10. Leningrad — 1 Mt Air Burst

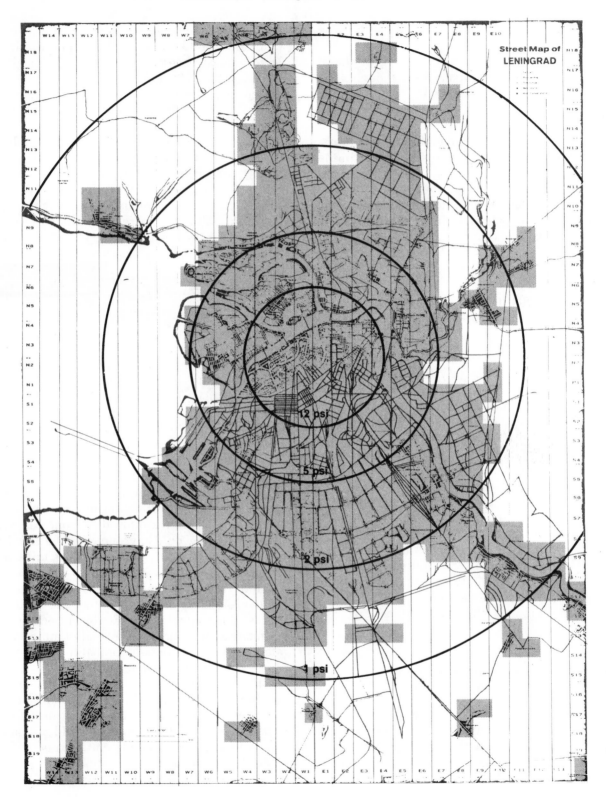

FIGURE 11.　Leningrad — 9 Mt Air Burst

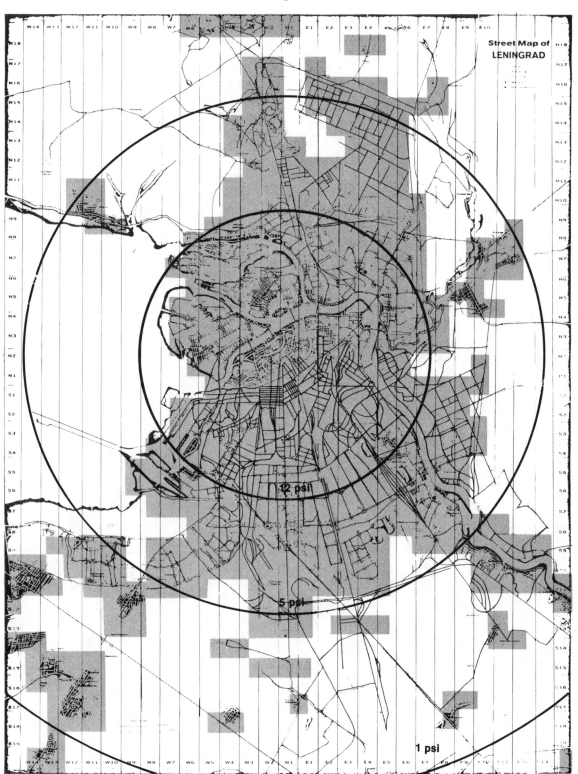

FIGURE 12.   Leningrad — Ten 40 kt Air Bursts

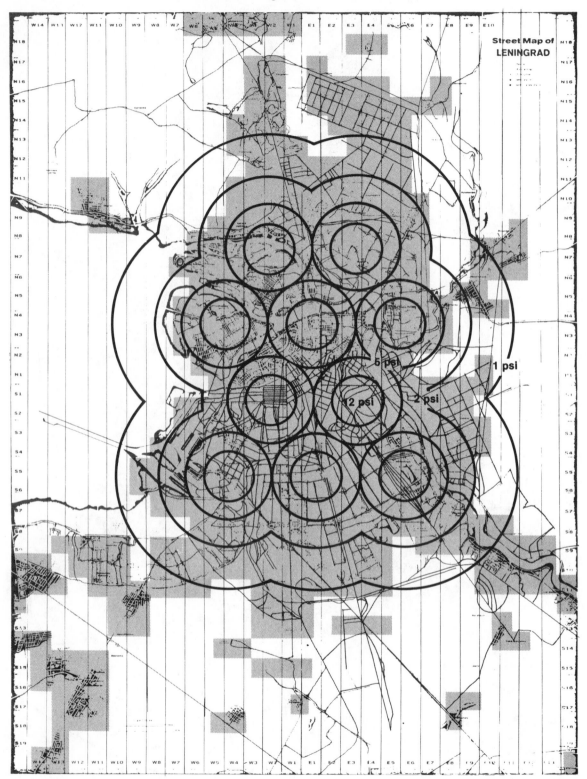

THE EFFECTS OF NUCLEAR WEAPONS 67

ings in a block, it is expected that 600 rems will reach out no further than 800 feet [245 m], thus covering an area only one-tenth as large. The thermal radiation will affect only those directly exposed up and down the street, while most people will be protected by buildings. Similarly, directly initiated fires will be insignificant, but the problem of secondary fires starting from building damage will remain. The local fallout pattern also will be highly distorted by the presence of the buildings. The fireball, confined between the buildings, will rise to a higher altitude than otherwise expected, leading to reduced local fallout but causing broadly distributed long-term fallout.

In summary, nuclear effects from a low-yield explosion in the confined space of an urban environment will differ significantly from large-yield effects, but in ways that are very difficult to estimate. Thus, the numbers of people and areas of buildings affected are very uncertain. However, it appears that, with the exception of streets directly exposed to the weapon, lethal ranges to people will be smaller than anticipated and dominated by the blast-induced collapse of nearby buildings.

4

Civil Defense Measures

Effective civil defense measures have the potential to reduce drastically the casualties and economic damage in the short term and to speed a nation's economic recovery in the long term. Civil defense seeks to preserve lives, economic capacity, post-attack viability, and pre-attack institutions and values. How far specific civil defense measures would succeed in doing so is controversial. Some observers argue that U.S. civil defense promotes deterrence by increasing the credibility of U.S. retaliation and by reducing any Soviet "destructive advantage" in a nuclear war. Others, however, argue that a vigorous civil defense program would induce people to believe that a nuclear war was "survivable" rather than "unthinkable," and that such a change in attitude would increase the risk of war.

POPULATION PROTECTION

People near potential targets must either seek protective shelter or evacuate these threatened areas and move to safer surroundings. If not at risk from immediate effects, they must still protect themselves from fallout. Both forms of protection depend on warning, shelter, supplies, life-support equipment (e.g., air filtration, toilets, communication devices), instruction, public health measures, and provision for rescue operations. In addition, evacuation involves transportation.

Blast Shelters

Some structures, particularly those designed for the purpose, offer substantial protection against direct nuclear effects (blast, thermal radiation, ionizing radiation, and induced fires). Since blast is usually the most difficult effect to protect against, such shelters are generally evaluated on blast resistance, and protection against other direct effects is assumed. Since most urban targets can be destroyed by an overpressure of 5 to 10 psi, a shelter providing protection against an overpressure of about 10 psi is called a *blast shelter,* although many blast shelters offer greater protection. Other shelters provide good protection against fallout, but little resistance to blast. Such "fallout shelters" are discussed in the next section. Blast shelters generally protect against fallout, but best meet this purpose when they contain adequate life-support systems. For example, a subway station without special provisions for water and ventilation would make a good blast shelter but a poor fallout shelter.

If the overpressure at a given spot is very low, a blast shelter is unnecessary; if the overpressure is very high (e.g., a direct hit with a surface burst), even the strongest blast shelters will fail. The "harder" the blast shelter (that is, the greater the overpressure it can withstand), the greater the area in which it could save its occupants' lives. Moreover, if the weapon height of burst is chosen to maximize the area receiving 5 to 10 psi, only a very small area (or no area at all) receives more than 40 to 50 psi. Hence, to attack blast shelters of

40 to 50 psi (which is a reasonably attainable hardness), weapons must be detonated at a lower altitude, reducing the area over which homes, buildings, and factories are destroyed.

The cost of a blast shelter depends on the extent of protection afforded and whether the shelter is detached or part of a building constructed for other purposes. The installation of shelters in new construction, or "slanting," is preferable, but it could take as long as 20 years for a national policy of slanting to provide adequate protection in cities.

An inexpensive way to protect a population from nuclear blast is to use existing underground facilities such as subways, where people can protect themselves for short periods. If people must remain in shelters to escape fallout, however, they will need life-support measures that require special preparation.

Other lethal nuclear effects cannot be overlooked. Although blast shelters usually protect against direct nuclear radiation, the shelters must be designed to ensure this end.

Fallout Shelters

If a sheltered population is to survive fallout, two things must be done. First, fallout must be prevented from infiltrating shelters through doors, ventilation, and other conduits. Measures must also be taken to prevent fallout from being tracked or carried into a shelter. More important, the shelter must allow its occupants to stay inside as long as outside radiation remains dangerous. Radiation doses are cumulative, and a few brief exposures to outside fallout may be far more hazardous than constant exposure to a low level of radiation that might penetrate a shelter.

Since radiation can remain dangerous for periods of a few days to several weeks, each shelter must be equipped to support its occupants for that amount of time. Requirements include adequate stocks of food, water, and necessary medical supplies and sanitary facilities. Equipment for controlling temperature, humidity, and air quality is also critical. With many people enclosed in an airtight shelter, temperatures, humidity, and carbon dioxide content increase, oxygen availability decreases, and fetid materials accumulate. Surface fires, naturally hot or humid weather, or crowded conditions may make things worse. If unregulated, slight increases in heat and humidity quickly lead to discomfort; substantial rises in temperature, humidity, and carbon dioxide could even cause death. Fires are also a threat to people in shelters because of extreme temperatures (possibly exceeding 2,000°F), carbon monoxide, and other noxious gases. A large fire might draw oxygen out of a shelter, suffocating shelterees.

In the United States, fallout shelters have been identified predominantly in urban areas by the Defense Civil Preparedness Agency (DCPA) shelter survey. These shelters are meant to protect against fallout from distant explosions (e.g., a Soviet attack on U.S. intercontinental ballistic missiles). On the other hand, Soviet fallout shelters are primarily intended for the rural population and an evacuated urban population.

Fallout protection is relatively easy to achieve. Any shielding material reduces the radiation intensity; various materials reduce the intensity by different amounts. In general, heavy, dense materials are better than light materials. And the greater the thickness of any one material, the greater the total reduction. The thicknesses of several common materials needed to reduce nuclear gamma radiation by a factor of 10 are listed below.

Shielding Effectiveness of Various Materials

Material	Thickness* (inches)
steel	4
concrete	12
earth	18
water	26
wood	50

*the thickness in inches needed to reduce nuclear gamma radiation by a factor of ten.

The amount of reduction, from outside levels to those inside, resulting from any particular choice and thickness of shielding material is called its *protection factor* (PF). For example, the thickness of each material listed above will provide a protection factor of 10. Consider an average home

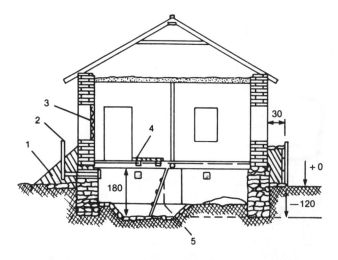

Basement of a stone house adapted for shelter: (1) earth embankment; (2) exhaust duct; (3) curtains on windows; (4) airtight hatch; (5) recessed pit.

basement that provides a protection factor of 10. Without additional protection, a family sheltered here could still be exposed to dangerous levels of radiation over time. For example, after 7 days an accumulated dose of almost 400 rems would occur inside the basement if the radiation outside totaled 4,000 roentgens. This could be attenuated to a relatively safe accumulation of 40 rems, if an additional 18 inches of dirt could be piled against windows and exposed walls before the fallout began. Thirty-six inches of dirt would reduce the dose to a negligible level of 4 rems (400 ÷ 100). Thus, as DCPA notes, "fallout protection is as cheap as dirt." But moving dry, unfrozen earth to increase the protection in a fallout shelter requires considerable time and effort, if done by hand. A cubic foot of earth weighs about 100 lb; a cubic yard about 2,700 lb.

The overall effectiveness of fallout shelters, therefore, depends on:

- having an adequate shelter — or enough time, information, and materials to build or improvise one;
- having sufficient food, water, and other supplies to enable people in the shelter to stay there until the outside fallout decays to a safe

level; depending on fallout intensity, this period may be as short as a few days or as long as a month;

- entering the shelter promptly before absorbing much radiation.

An individual caught by fallout before reaching shelter may not be able to enter a shelter without contaminating it.

Over the years, home fallout shelters have received considerable attention. The government has distributed plans for making home basements better shelters. Such plans typically involve piling dirt against windows and, if possible, on floors above the shelter area, stocking provisions, obtaining radios and batteries, and building makeshift toilets. These simple actions can substantially increase protection against radiation and may slightly improve protection against blast. However, few homes in the South and West have basements.

With adequate time, instructions, and materials, an *expedient shelter* offering reasonable radiation protection can be constructed. This is a buried or semiburied structure, shielded from radiation by dirt and other common materials. Expedient shelter construction figures prominently in Soviet civil defense planning.

Evacuation

Evacuation is conceptually simple: People move from high-risk to low-risk areas. In effect, evacuation (or *crisis relocation*) uses safe distances for protection from immediate nuclear effects. The effectiveness of crisis relocation is highly scenario dependent. If relocated people have time to find or build shelters, if the areas into which people evacuate do not become new targets, and if evacuated targets are attacked, evacuation can save many lives.

Although evacuation is far cheaper per capita than constructing blast shelters, planning and implementing an evacuation is difficult. First, people must be organized and transported to relocation areas — a staggering logistics problem. Unless people go to specific, assigned relocation areas, many areas could be overwhelmed with evacuees, causing severe health and safety problems. Unless private transportation is strictly controlled, monumental traffic jams could result. Unless adequate public transportation is provided, many people would be stranded in blast areas. Unless there are necessary supplies at relocation areas, people might rebel against authority. Unless medical care is available at relocation areas, health problems would multiply.

Once evacuated, people must be sheltered. They might be assigned to existing public shelters or to private homes with basements suitable for shelter. If materials are available and time permits, new public shelters could be built. Evacuees would require many of the same life-support functions described previously under fallout shelters; providing these in sufficient quantity would be difficult.

Evacuation entails many unknowns. The time available for evacuation is unknown, but extremely critical. People should be evacuated to areas that will receive little fallout, yet fallout deposition areas cannot be accurately predicted. Crisis relocation could increase the perceived threat of nuclear war and even help to destabilize a crisis.

Whether and how people would obey an evacuation order would depend on many factors, especially public perception of a deteriorating international crisis. If an evacuation were ordered and people were willing to comply with it, would time allow compliance? If the attack came while the evacuation was underway, more people might die than if evacuation had not been attempted. A sufficient warning depends on circumstances; a U.S. President might order an evacuation only if the Soviets had started one. In this case, the United States might have less evacuation time than the Soviets. The abundance of transportation in the United States could in theory permit faster evacuation, but panic, traffic jams, and inadequate planning could nullify this advantage. Disorder and panic, should they occur, would impede evacuation.

The success of evacuation in the United States would probably vary from region to region. Generally, evacuation requires little planning in sparsely populated areas. In some areas, especially the Midwest and South, evacuation is feasible but would require special planning because of fallout from attacks on ICBM silos. The broad swaths of intense fallout would require that people travel much further to avoid them. Evacuation from the densely populated Boston-to-Washington and Sacramento-to-San Diego corridors, with their tens of millions of people and limited relocation areas, could prove impossible.

The Soviet Union reportedly has plans for large-scale evacuation of cities, and debate on its effectiveness has stimulated discussion of a similar plan for the United States. But tactical warning of a missile attack does not give enough time for an evacuation. Evacuation plans thus assume that an intense crisis will provide several days' strategic warning of an attack and that the leadership will make use of this warning.

Evacuation involves considerably more pre-attack planning than a shelter-based civil defense plan, because logistic and other organizational requirements for moving millions of people in a few days are much more complex. Plans must be made to care for the relocated people. People must know where to go. Transportation or evacuation routes must be provided. A survey of the U.S. population revealed that many would spontaneously evacuate in a severe crisis, which could interfere with a planned evacuation.

Some U.S. analysts argue that detailed Soviet evacuation plans, together with evidence of practical evacuation preparations, indicate a reasonable evacuation capability. Others claim that actual Soviet capabilities are far less than those suggested in official plans and that an actual evacuation under crisis conditions would result in a mixture of evacuation according to plan for some, delay for others, and utter chaos in some places. In any case, a large evacuation has never been attempted in the United States. The extent of Soviet evacuation exercises is controversial.

Crisis relocation of large populations would have major economic impacts. These are the subject of a Defense Civil Preparedness Agency study in which the Treasury, Federal Reserve Board, and Federal Preparedness Agency are participating. Results indicate that economic impacts of relocation, followed by crisis resolution and re-

turn of evacuees, could continue for 1 to 3 years, but that appropriate government policies could significantly reduce such impacts. If blast shelters for key workers are built in high-risk areas, and if workers are willing to accept these risks, essential industries could be kept functioning while most people were in relocation areas. Such a program would substantially reduce the economic impacts of an extended crisis relocation.

PROTECTION OF ECONOMIC RESOURCES

Efforts to preserve critical economic assets, and thereby accelerate post-attack recovery, could take several forms. For example, if there is warning, railroad rolling stock might be moved from urban yards into rural locations, perhaps saving many cars and their cargo. Some industrial equipment and tooling might be protected by burial and sandbagging. Other industrial facilities, such as petroleum refineries and chemical plants, may be impossible to protect. Industrial defense measures include making buildings or machinery more resistant to blast pressure (hardening), dispersal of individual sites and mobile assets (e.g., transport, tools, equipment, fuel), proliferation of redundant and complementary capabilities, and plans to minimize disruption to an economy and its components in wartime by coordinated shutdown of industrial processes, speedy damage control, and plant repair.

There is no feasible way to protect an industrial facility that is targeted by a nuclear weapon with 1980s accuracy. Protective measures might, however, be helpful at industrial facilities that are merely close to targets.

Some equipment within structures can be protected against blast, fire, and debris. Costly, critical equipment and finished products can be sheltered in semiburied structures and other protective facilities. A recent study[1] demonstrated that special hardening measures could save some machinery at blast overpressures that would destroy the building in which the machinery is housed. However, it is unknown whether the amount of equipment that could actually be protected would make much difference in recovery.

Another method of protecting industrial capabilities is the maintenance of stockpiles of critical equipment and finished goods. Stockpiling will not provide a continuing supply of the stockpiled goods, but could ensure the availability of critical items until their production could be resumed. Stockpiles can be targeted if their locations are known. They could also suffer damage by being close to targets.

Finally, dispersal of industry, both between facilities and within a facility consisting of several buildings, can decrease damage to buildings from weapons aimed at other buildings. A Soviet text on civil defense notes that:

> Measures may be taken nationally to limit the concentration of industry in certain regions. A rational and dispersed location of industries in the territories of our country is of great national economic importance, primarily from the standpoint of an accelerated economic development, but also from the standpoint of organizing protection from weapons of mass destruction.[2]

However, there is little evidence that the U.S.S.R. has adopted industrial dispersion as national policy. Despite reports of industrial decentralization over the last decade or so, Soviet industry appears more concentrated than ever. An excellent example is the Kama River truck and auto facility, a giant complex the size of Manhattan Island that produces one-fifth of all Soviet motor vehicles. Clearly, Soviet planners have chosen industrial efficiency and economies of scale over civil defense considerations. Similarly, the United States has no policy of decentralization, and other facts suggest that the possibility of nuclear war is not a significant civil planning determinant. There are those who reason that this disregard for many of the consequences of nuclear war indicates that policymakers believe nuclear war is very unlikely.

The economic and social problems following a nuclear attack cannot be foreseen clearly enough to permit drafting of detailed recovery plans. However, plans can be made to preserve the continuity of government, and both the United States and the Soviet Union have such plans.

U.S. CIVIL DEFENSE

U.S. attitudes about civil defense have been ambivalent ever since the Federal Civil Defense Act of 1950 responded to the first Soviet test of an atomic bomb. Indeed, much of U.S. civil defense was a reaction to external factors rather than part of a carefully thought through program. The "duck and cover" program and the evacuation route program, both of the early 1950s, responded to the threat of Soviet atomic bombs carried by manned bombers. Lack of suitable protection against fire and blast led to plans for rapid evacuation of cities during the several hours separating radar warning and the arrival of Soviet bombers.

The first Soviet test of thermonuclear weapons in 1953 necessitated changes in these plans. The higher yield of these weapons meant that short-distance evacuations and modestly hard blast shelters in cities would provide no protection and that simply ducking in school corridors, while perhaps better than nothing, was not part of a serious civil defense plan.

H-bombs also raised the specter of radioactive fallout blanketing large areas of the country. Previously, civil defense consisted of moving people a short distance out of cities, while the rest of the country remained unscathed and able to help the target cities. However, large-scale fallout meant that large, unpredictable areas of the country would become contaminated, people would be forced to take shelter in those areas, and thus pinned down, would be unable to offer much help to attacked cities for several weeks. The advent of ICBMs necessitated further changes. Their drastically reduced warning times precluded evacuations based on radar warning of attack.

With previous plans made useless, the United States cast around for alternative plans. One approach was to identify and stock fallout shelters, while recognizing the impracticability of protecting people from blast. After the Berlin crisis of 1961, President Kennedy initiated a program to provide fallout shelters for the entire population. The National Shelter Survey Program proposed:

- the survey, identification, and stocking of existing shelters;

- the subsidization of fallout shelter installation in new construction;
- the construction of single-purpose fallout shelters where these were needed.

Only the first step in this program was ever authorized. The government also urged people to build home fallout shelters.

In the early 1970s the civil defense program was broadened to include preparedness for peacetime as well as wartime disasters. The 1970s also saw a new emphasis on operational capabilities of all available assets, including warning systems, shelters, radiological detection instruments and trained personnel, police and firefighting forces, doctors and hospitals, and experienced management. This development program was called On-Site Assistance.

The mid-1970s saw the initiation of contingency planning to evacuate city and other high-risk populations during a period of severe crisis. At present, U.S. civil defense has the following plans and capabilities:

Organization. The federal civil defense function has been repeatedly reorganized since the Federal Civil Defense Act of 1950. The most recent organization gave prime responsibility for civil defense to the Defense Civil Preparedness Agency (DCPA), housed in the Defense Department. The Federal Preparedness Agency (FPA) in the General Services Administration conducts some planning for peacetime nuclear emergencies, economic crises, continuity of government following a nuclear attack, and other emergencies. The Federal Disaster Assistance Administration (FDAA), in the Department of Housing and Urban Development, is concerned with peacetime disaster response. In 1978, Congress assented to a Presidential proposal to reorganize civil defense and peacetime disaster functions into a single agency, the Federal Emergency Management Agency, which incorporates DCPA, FPA, FDAA, and other agencies.

Civil protection. The United States is looking increasingly at crisis relocation, under which city dwellers would move to rural "host" areas when an attack appeared likely. Because it would require several days of warning, crisis relocation would be carried out during a crisis rather than on radar warning of missile launch. The United States has conducted surveys to identify potential fallout shelters in host areas, and blast and fallout shelters in high-risk areas. Through FY 1971, about 118,000 buildings were marked as shelters; about 95,000 other buildings were identified as potential shelters but have not been marked. Marking would be done in crises. In the early 1960s, the federal government purchased austere survival supplies for shelters. The shelf life of these supplies has expired; shelter stocking is now to be accomplished during a crisis.

Direction and control. The federal government has several teletype, voice, and radio systems for communicating during crises between DCPA, FDAA, and FPA headquarters, regional offices, states, and Canada. State and local governments are planning to integrate communication systems into this net. DCPA has eight regions, each with emergency operating centers (EOCs). Six of these centers are hardened against nuclear blast. Forty-three States have EOCs, and EOCs with fallout protection are operational or under development in locales that include about half the population.

Attack warning. The National Warning System can transmit a warning to over 1,200 federal, state, and local warning points, which operate 24 hours a day. Once warning has reached local levels, it is passed on to the public by sirens or other means. Almost half of the U.S. population is in areas that could receive outdoor warning within 15 minutes of the issue of a national warning. However, dissemination of warnings is inadequate in many places.

Emergency public information. Fallout protection, emergency power generators, and remote units have been provided for radio stations in the Emergency Broadcast System, to permit broadcast of emergency information under fallout conditions. About a third of the stations are in high-risk areas and could be destroyed by blast. A program has been initiated to protect 180 stations from electromagnetic pulse. About one-third of the more than 5,000 localities participating in the civil defense program have reported development of plans to provide the public with information in emergencies.

Radiological defense. This function encompasses radiological detection instruments, communication, plans and procedures, and personnel trained to detect and evaluate radiological hazards. Between 1955 and 1975, the federal government procured about 1.4 million rate meters, 3.4 million dose meters, and related equipment. Effective radiological defense would require an estimated 2.4 million people to be trained as radiological monitors in a crisis.

Citizen training. The civil defense program once provided substantial training for the public at large, but crisis training via news media must now be relied on to educate citizens on hazards and survival actions. DCPA offers classroom and home study training for civil defense personnel.

On paper, civil defense looks effective. The United States has more than enough identified fallout shelter spaces for the entire population, which include underground parking, subways, tunnels, and deep basement potential blast shelters. It has a vast network of highways and vehicles; every holiday weekend sees a substantial urban evacuation. CB and other radios can aid communication after an attack. The United States also has enormous resources (food, medical supplies, electrical-generating capability) beyond the minimum needed for survival.

Despite all these considerations, however, no one is convinced that the United States has an effective civil defense. U.S. Civil defense capability is weakened by the fact that some elements are in place while others are not or have not been maintained. Shelters will not support life if their occupants have no water. Evacuation plans will save fewer people if host areas have inadequate shelter spaces and supplies, or if people are poorly distributed among towns. Faced with drastic technological change, moral and philosophical questions about the desirability of civil defense, and budgetary constraints, federal plans have been marked by vacillation, shifts in direction, and endless reorganization.

SOVIET CIVIL DEFENSE

Soviet civil defense has faced the same technical challenges as the United States — atomic bombs, hydrogen bombs, fallout, ICBMs, limited warning, and so on. The Soviet Union has consistently devoted more resources to civil defense than has the United States, and has been more willing to make and follow long-term plans. However, it is not known how Soviet leaders evaluate the effectiveness of their civil defense.

The Soviet civil defense organization is a part of the Ministry of Defense. Permanent full-time staff of the organization is believed to number over 100,000. Some civil defense training is compulsory for all Soviet citizens, and many study first aid. There has also been a large shelter-building program.

The Soviets reportedly have an extensive urban evacuation plan. Each urban resident is assigned to a specific evacuation area. Such areas are located on collective farms, and each farmer has instructions and a list of the people he or she is to receive. If fallout protection were not available, simple expedient shelters would be constructed quickly. Soviet plans recommend that shelters be located at least 40 km [24 miles] from the city to provide sufficient protection against the effects of a 1 Mt weapon exploding at an altitude of 10 to 20 km [6 to 12 miles].

In July 1978, the Central Intelligence Agency (CIA) released its unclassified study, *Soviet Civil Defense.*[3] In brief, the report finds that Soviet civil defense is "an ongoing nationwide program under military control." It notes several motivations for the program: to convince potential adversaries they cannot defeat the Soviet Union, to increase Soviet strength should war occur, to help maintain the logistics base for continuing a war effort following nuclear attack, to save people and resources, and to promote post-attack recovery. The report observes that Soviet civil defense "is not a crash effort, but its pace increased beginning in the late 1960s." It points to several difficulties with the program: bureaucratic problems, apathy, little protection of factories, and little dispersal of industry.

According to the report, the specific goals of Soviet civil defense are to protect the leadership, essential workers, and others (in that order); to protect productivity; and to sustain people and prepare for economic recovery following an attack. In assessing Soviet efforts to meet these goals, the CIA found:

The Soviets probably have sufficient blast-shelter space in hardened command posts for virtually all the leadership elements at all levels (about 110,000 people) . . . . Shelters at key economic installations could accommodate about 12 to 24 percent of the total work force . . . .

A minimum of 10 to 20 percent of the total population in urban areas (including essential workers) could be accommodated at present in blast-resistant shelters.

The critical decision to be made by the Soviet leaders in terms of sparing the population would be whether or not to evacuate cities. Only by evacuating the bulk of the urban population could they hope to achieve a marked reduction in the number of urban casualties. An evacuation of urban areas could probably be accomplished in two or three days, with as much as a week required for full evacuation of the largest cities . . . .

Soviet measures to protect the economy could not prevent massive industrial damage . . . .

[Regarding post-attack recovery], the coordination of requirements with available supplies and transportation is a complex problem for Soviet planners even in peacetime, let alone following a large-scale nuclear attack.[3]

Assessing the effectiveness of Soviet civil defense, the CIA study found that a worst-case attack could kill or injure well over 100 million people, but many leaders would survive. With a few days to evacuate and provide shelter, casualties could be reduced by more than 50 percent. With a week for pre-attack planning, "Soviet civil defenses could reduce casualties to the low tens of millions."

The U.S. Arms Control and Disarmament Agency (ACDA) released *An Analysis of Civil Defense in Nuclear War* in December 1978.[4] This study concluded that Soviet civil defense could do little to mitigate the effects of a major attack. Blast shelters might reduce fatalities to 80 percent of those in an unsheltered case, but this could be offset by targeting additional weapons (e.g., those on bombers and submarines that would be alerted during a crisis) against cities.

Evacuation might reduce fatalities to a range of 25 million to 35 million, but if the United States were to target the evacuated population, some 50 million might be killed. Furthermore, civil defense could do little to protect the Soviet economy, so millions of evacuees and injured could not be supported after the attack ended.

The sharp disagreement about Soviet civil defense capability revolves around several key issues:

- Can the Soviets follow their stated civil defense plans?
- How widely would evacuees be dispersed?
- How well would evacuees be protected from fallout?
- How effective is Soviet industrial hardening?

The uncertainties involved in answering these questions lead to wide discrepancies in reported estimates of the effects of an all-out nuclear attack on the Soviet Union.

CONCLUDING REMARKS

We have provided a brief description of civil defense measures that might mitigate the impact of nuclear war. However, no effort has been made to answer the following key questions:

- Would a civil defense program on a large scale make a big difference, or only a marginal difference, in the impact of a nuclear war on civil society?
- What impact would various kinds of civil defense measures have on peacetime diplomacy or crisis stability?
- What civil defense measures would be appropriate if nuclear war were considered likely in the next few years?
- What kind and size of civil defense program might be worth the money it would cost?

The answers to these questions are beyond the scope of this book.

5

Three Nuclear Attack Cases

This chapter presents descriptions of three different "cases" of nuclear attack. These cases do not necessarily represent "probable" kinds of nuclear attacks; they were chosen to illustrate the different effects various types of attacks could have on the civilian population, economy, and society. Moreover, each case is considered in isolation—events that could lead up to such an attack are deliberately ignored, because their prediction is impossible. And it is assumed (although the assumption is questionable at best) that the attack described is not followed by further nuclear attacks.

Each case considers first a Soviet attack on the United States, and then a U.S. attack on the Soviet Union. These attacks involve similar kinds of targets, but differ in detail because both the weapons available to the attacker and the geography of the victim are different. This discussion does not suggest that a real attack would be followed by a mirror-image retaliation; rather, it looks at similar attacks in order to highlight the asymmetries of vulnerability in the United States and the Soviet Union.

The following analyses are more like sketches than detailed illustrations. Precise prediction of the future of the United States or the Soviet Union is impossible—even without accounting for something as unprecedented as a nuclear attack. A detailed study would say more about the assumptions used than about the impacts of nuclear war. This book indicates the kinds of effects that would probably be most significant and comments on the major uncertainties.

The three cases of nuclear attack considered include a "limited" attack on industrial targets, a large counterforce attack, and a massive, all-out attack.

A "limited" attack on industrial targets. Here, the hypothetical attack was limited to ten strategic nuclear delivery vehicles (SNDVs)—Soviet SS-18 intercontinental ballistic missiles (ICBMs), U.S. Poseidon submarine-launched ballistic missiles (SLBMs), and Minuteman III ICBMs. Oil refining was chosen as the hypothetical target because it is vital, vulnerable, and concentrated in both countries. It was assumed that the attack would be planned with no effort to minimize or maximize civilian casualties.

A large counterforce attack. The possibilities considered included both an attack on ICBM silos only (a case that has gained some notoriety as a result of assertions by some that the United States may become vulnerable to such an attack) and an attack on silos, missile submarine bases, and bomber bases (which some characterize as the least irrational way to wage a strategic nuclear war). The analysis draws on several previous studies that made varying assumptions about attack design, weapon size, targets attacked, and vulnerability of the population. The ways in which variations in these assumptions affect estimated fatalities are discussed.

A massive, all-out attack. This description of an attack against a full range of military and economic targets is intended to approximate "the ultimate deterrent"—the climax of an escalation process—and draws on several previous studies that made differing assumptions about the number of weapons used and the precise choice of targets. Such variations are useful in indicating the range of possibilities. However, deliberate efforts to kill as many people as possible are not assumed. Such efforts would cause 10 to 20 million more immediate deaths than targeting economic and military facilities.

A SOVIET ATTACK ON U.S. OIL REFINERIES

As far as we know, this kind of nuclear attack—a "limited" attack on economic targets—has not been studied elsewhere in recent years. This section investigates what might happen if the Soviet Union attempted to inflict as much economic damage as possible with an attack limited to ten SNDVs, in this case ten SS-18 ICBMs carrying multiple, independently targetable reentry vehicles (MIRVs). An OTA contractor designed such an attack, operating on instructions to limit the attack to ten missiles, to create hypothetical economic damage that would take a very long time to repair, and to design the attack without any effort either to maximize or to minimize human casualties. The Department of Defense (DOD) then calculated the immediate results of this hypothetical attack, using the same data base, methodology, and assumptions it uses for its own studies.

Given the limitation of ten ICBMs, the most vulnerable element of the U.S. economy was judged to be the energy supply system. The number of separate components in this system forces the selection of a system subset that is critical, vulnerable to a small attack, and impossible to repair or replace in a short period (Table 6).

OTA and the contractor jointly determined that petroleum refining facilities most nearly met these criteria. The United States has about 300 major refineries, and refineries are relatively vulnerable to damage from nuclear blasts. The key production components are the distillation units, cracking units, cooling towers, power house, and boiler plant. Fractionating towers, the most vulnerable components of the distillation and cracking units, collapse and overturn in relatively low winds and overpressures. Storage tanks can be lifted from their foundations by similar effects, incurring severe damage and loss of contents and raising the probability of secondary fires and explosions.

MIRVed missiles are used to maximize damage per missile. The attack consists of eight 1 Mt warheads on each of ten SS-18 ICBMs, a reasonable choice given the objective of the attack. Like all MIRVed missiles, the SS-18 has limitations of *footprint*—the area within which the warheads from a single missile can be aimed. Thus, the Soviets could strike not any 80 refineries but only 8 targets in each of 10 footprints of roughly 125,000 square miles [32 million hectares]. The footprint

TABLE 6.   Energy Production and Distribution Components

Category	Prime sources	Numbers	Processing	Numbers	Distribution
Oil	Wells	Thousands	Refineries	Tens/hundreds (tend to be clustered)	Pipelines/rail/truck/barge/ship
	Ports (imports) Pipelines (imports)	Tens			
Gas	Wells	Thousands	Gas plants	Tens/hundreds	Pipelines/rail/truck/barge/ship
	Oil refineries	Hundreds			
	Ports (imports)	Tens	Deliquification plants	Tens	
	Pipelines (imports)	Tens			
Coal	Mines	Hundreds	Usually at mines	Hundreds	Rail/truck/barge/coal slurry pipelines
Electric power production	Hydroelectric	Tens	Same as prime source		Powerlines/power grids
	Thermal	Hundreds			
	Nuclear power	Tens			
	Power grids (imports)	Units			

SOURCES: *Vulnerability of Total Petroleum Systems* (Washington, D.C.: Department of the Interior, Office of Oil and Gas), May 1973, prepared for the Defense Civil Preparedness Agency.
National Energy Outlook: 1976 (Washington, D.C.: Federal Energy Administration), February 1976.

Baytown refinery, Texas

FIGURE 13.   Approximate Footprint Coverages

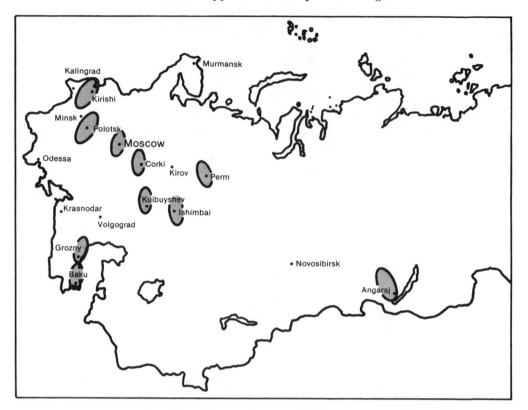

U.S. attack on Soviet Union

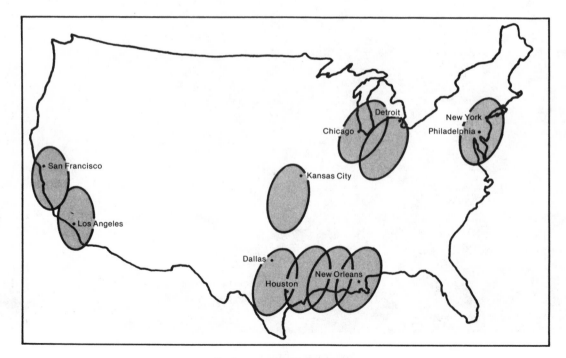

Soviet attack on United States

size and the tendency of U.S. refineries to be located in clusters near major cities, however, make the SS-18 appropriate. The footprints are shown in Figure 13. Table 7 lists U.S. refineries by capacity. Table 8 lists the percentage of U.S. refining capacity destroyed in each footprint.

The attack consists of 80 1 Mt weapons; it strikes the 77 refineries having the largest capacity and uses the 3 remaining warheads as second weapons on the largest refineries in the appropriate missile footprints. Each weapon that detonates over a refinery is assumed to destroy its target. This assumption is reasonable in view of

the vulnerability of refineries and the fact that a 1 Mt weapon produces 5 psi overpressure out to about 4.3 miles [6.9 km]. Thus, damage to refineries is mainly a function of numbers of weapons, not their yield or accuracy; collateral damage, however, is affected by all three factors. It is also assumed that every warhead detonates over its target. But some weapons would not explode or would be off course. The Soviets could, however, compensate for failures of launch vehicles by readying more than ten ICBMs for the attack and programming missiles to replace any failures in the initial ten. Finally, all weapons are assumed

TABLE 7.   U.S. Refinery Locations and Refining Capacity

Rank order	Location	Percent capacity	Cumulative percent capacity	Rank order	Location	Percent capacity	Cumulative percent capacity
1	Baytown, Tex.	3.6	3.6	34	Avon, Calif.	0.7	47.9
2	Baton Rouge, La.	2.9	6.4	35	Toledo, Ohio	0.7	48.6
3	El Segundo, Calif.	2.3	8.7	36	Corpus Christi, Tex.	0.7	49.3
4	Whiting, Ind.	2.1	10.8	37	Torrence, Calif.	0.7	50.0
5	Port Arthur, Tex.	2.1	12.9	38	Nederland, Tex.	0.7	50.6
6	Richmond, Calif.	2.0	14.9	39	Toledo, Ohio	0.7	51.3
7	Texas City, Tex.	2.0	16.9	40	Port Arthur, Tex.	0.6	51.9
8	Beaumont, Tex.	1.9	18.8	41	Wilmington, Calif.	0.6	52.5
9	Port Arthur, Tex.	1.9	20.7	42	Sugar Creek, Mo.	0.6	53.1
10	Houston, Tex.	1.8	22.5	43	Ferndale, Wash.	0.6	53.7
11	Linden, N.J.	1.6	24.1	44	Sweeny, Tex.	0.6	54.3
12	Deer Park, Tex.	1.6	25.7	45	Borger, Tex.	0.6	54.9
13	Wood River, Ill.	1.5	27.3	46	Paulsboro, N.J.	0.5	55.4
14	Pasagoula, Miss.	1.6	28.9	47	Wood River, Ill.	0.5	55.9
15	Norco, La.	1.3	30.1	48	Benicia, Calif.	0.5	56.5
16	Philadelphia, Pa.	1.2	31.3	49	Wilmington, Calif.	0.5	57.0
17	Garyville, La.	1.1	32.4	50	Martinez, Calif.	0.5	57.5
18	Belle Chasse, La.	1.1	33.5	51	Anacortes, Wash.	0.5	58.0
19	Robinson, Tex.	1.1	34.6	52	Kansas City, Kans.	0.5	58.5
20	Corpus Christi, Tex.	1.0	35.7	53	Tulsa, Okla.	0.5	59.0
21	Philadelphia, Pa.	1.0	36.7	54	Westville, N.J.	0.5	59.5
22	Joliett, Ill.	1.0	37.7	55	West Lake, La.	0.5	60.0
23	Carson, Calif.	1.0	38.7	56	Lawrenceville, Ill.	0.5	60.4
24	Lima, Ohio	0.9	39.6	57	Eldorado, Kans.	0.5	60.9
25	Perth Amboy, N.J.	0.9	40.6	58	Meraux, La.	0.4	61.3
26	Marcus Hook, Pa.	0.9	41.5	59	El Paso, Tex.	0.4	61.7
27	Marcus Hook, Pa.	0.9	42.4	60	Wilmington, Calif.	0.4	62.2
28	Corpus Christi, Tex.	0.9	43.3	61	Virgin Islands/Guam[a]	4.1	66.3
29	Lemont, Tex.	0.8	44.1	62	Puerto Rico[a]	1.6	67.9
30	Convent, La.	0.8	44.9	63	Alaska[a]	0.5	68.4
31	Delaware City, Del.	0.8	45.7	64	Hawaii[a] [b]	0.3	68.7
32	Cattletsburg, Ky.	0.8	46.5	65	Other[c]	31.3	100.0
33	Ponca City, Okla.	0.7	47.2				

[a]Sum of all refineries in the indicated geographic area.
[b]Foreign trade zone only.
[c]Includes summary data from all refineries with capacity less than 75,000 bbl/day. 224 refineries included.
SOURCE: National Petroleum Refiners Association.

TABLE 8. Summary of U.S.S.R. Attack on the United States

Footprint number	Geographic area	EMT[a]	Percent national refining capacity	Percent national storage capacity	Air burst prompt fatalities (x 1,000)
1	Texas	8	14.9	NA[b]	472
2	Indiana, Illinois, Ohio	8	8.1	NA	365
3	New Jersey, Pennsylvania, Delaware	8	7.9	NA	845
4	California	8	7.8	NA	1,252
5	Louisiana, Texas, Mississippi	8	7.5	NA	377
6	Texas	8	4.5	NA	377
7	Illinois, Indiana, Michigan	8	3.6	NA	484
8	Louisiana	8	3.6	NA	278
9	Oklahoma, Kansas	8	3.3	NA	365
10	California	8	2.5	NA	357
	Totals	80	63.7	NA	5,031

[a]EMT = Equivalent megatons.
[b]NA = Not applicable.

detonated at an altitude that would maximize the area receiving an overpressure of at least 5 psi — enough to destroy refineries. Consequences of using ground bursts are noted where relevant.

Immediate Effects: The First Hour

The attack succeeds. The 80 weapons destroy 64 percent of U.S. petroleum refining capacity. The attack also causes much collateral, or unintended, damage. Its only goal was to maximize economic recovery time, but because of the high-yield weapons and the proximity of the refineries to large cities, the attack kills over 5 million people (see Table 8) if all weapons are air burst. Because no fireball touches the ground, this attack produces little fallout. If all weapons were ground burst, 2,883,000 fatalities and 312,000 fallout fatalities would result.

The Defense Civil Preparedness Agency (DCPA) provided fatality estimates for this attack by using the following assumptions regarding the protective postures of the population in its calculations:

- Ten percent of the population in large cities spontaneously evacuates beforehand due to rising tensions and crisis development.
- Home basements and public shelters such as subways are used as fallout shelters.

- People are distributed among fallout shelters that provide varying protection in proportion to the number of shelter spaces at each level of protection rather than occupying the best spaces first.
- The remaining people are in buildings that offer the same blast protection as a single-story home (2 to 3 psi); radiation protection factors are commensurate with the type of structures occupied.

Other uncertainties that affect the number of casualties and extent of damage include fires, panic, inaccurate reentry vehicles (RVs) that detonate off target, time of day, season, and local weather. Such uncertainties were not incorporated into the calculations, but have consequences noted in Chapter 3.

The attack also causes much collateral economic damage. Because many U.S. refineries are located near cities and because the Soviets use relatively large weapons, the attack destroys many buildings and other structures typical of any large city. The attack also destroys many economic facilities associated with refineries, such as railroads, pipelines, and petroleum storage tanks. While the attack leaves many U.S. ports unscathed, it damages many that are equipped to handle oil, greatly reducing U.S. petroleum importing capability. Similarly, many petrochemi-

TABLE 9.   Electric Powerplants in Philadelphia

Name	Capacity (kW)	Average usage kW (1976)	Distance from blast	
Schuylkill	249,000 steam + 36,750 internal combustion (I.C.)	111,630	1.3	Electrical equipment destroyed. Plant heavily damaged.
Southwark	356,000 steam + 66,750 I.C.	71,605	2.6	Electrical equipment damaged or destroyed. Plant moderately damaged.
Delaware	250,000 steam + 68,750 I.C.	162,799	4.9	Electrical equipment moderately damaged. Plant intact.
Richmond	275,000 steam + 63,400 I.C.	29,247	6.6	Probably undamaged.
Totals	1,130,000 kW (steam) + 235,650 I.C.	375,281		

SOURCE: *Electrical World: Directory of Electricial Utilities* (New York, N.Y.: McGraw Hill Inc., 1977).

cal plants use feedstocks from refineries, so most plants producing complex petrochemicals are located near refineries; indeed, 60 percent of the petrochemicals produced in the United States are made in Texas gulf coast plants.[1] Many of these plants are destroyed by the attack, and many others are idle for lack of feedstocks. In sum, the attack aimed only at refineries causes much damage to the entire petroleum industry and other assets as well.

Not all economic damage was calculated, because no existing data base would support reasonably accurate calculations. Instead, the issue is approached by using Philadelphia to illustrate the effects of the attack on large cities. Philadelphia contains two major refineries that supply much of the refined petroleum for the Northeast corridor. Each refinery is struck by a 1 Mt weapon (see Figure 14). Since other major U.S. cities are near targeted refineries, similar damage occurs in Houston, Los Angeles, and Chicago.

The Defense Civil Preparedness Agency (DCPA) provided estimates of the pre-blast populations of various zones and the number of people killed in each. These results are summarized in the following table for distances of 2 and 5 miles [3 and 8 km] from the detonations:

Deaths from Philadelphia Attack

Distance from detonation	Original population	Number killed	Percent killed
2 mi.	155,000	135,000	87
5 mi.	785,000	410,000	52

Detailed examination of the map of Philadelphia also indicates the magnitude of the problems and the resources available to cope with them. Local production, storage, and distribution of petroleum are destroyed. Besides the two refineries, nearly all of the oil storage tanks are in the immediate target area. Presumably, reserve supplies can be brought to Philadelphia from other areas unless — as is likely — they are also attacked. While early overland shipment by rail or tank truck into north and northeast Philadelphia should be possible, water transport up the Delaware River may not be. This busy, narrow channel passes within about 1.3 miles [2.1 km] of one of the targets and could become blocked at least temporarily by a grounded, heavily laden iron ore ship (bound upriver for the Fairless Works) or by sunken ships or barges.

There are four major electric powerplants in or near Philadelphia. Their capacity, average usage (1976), and expected damage are summarized in Table 9.

The usage figures are average and do not reflect peak demand, but a large percentage of this demand disappears with destruction of the industrial areas along the Schuylkill River and of a large portion of the downtown business district. Thus, the plant in the Richmond section of Philadelphia, may be able to handle the emergency load. Assuming early recovery of the Delaware plant, there probably will be adequate emergency electric power for the surviving portion of the distribution system.

FIGURE 14. Philadelphia and Surrounding Counties.

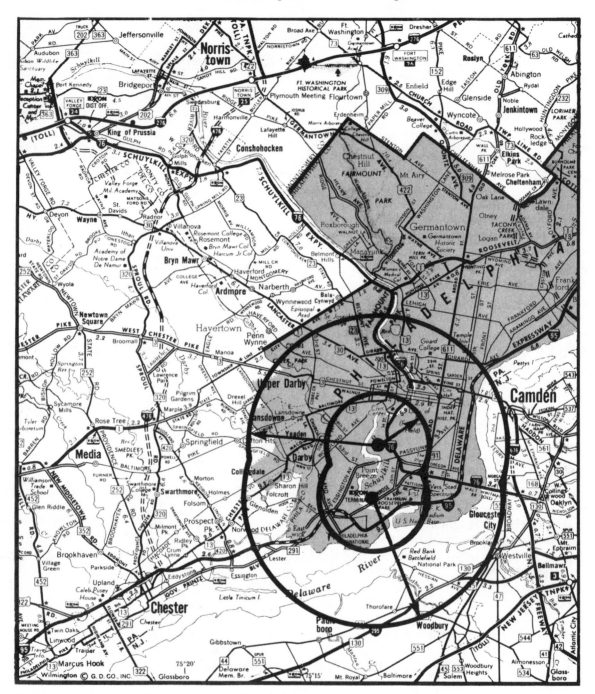

The two large dots represent the ground zeros of the two 1-Mt Soviet weapons. Within 2 miles of these ground zeros, there are approximately 155,000 people of which 135,000 were calculated to have been killed.

Transportation facilities are fairly hard hit by the attack:

Air. The major facilities of the Philadelphia International Airport are located about 1.7 miles [2.8 km] from the nearest burst. These are severely damaged. The runways are 1.7 to 2.9 miles [2.8 to 4.6 km] from the nearest burst and experience little or no long-term damage. Alternate airfields in the northeast and those near Camden, New Jersey are unaffected.

Rail. The main Conrail lines from Washington to New York and New England pass about a mile from the nearest burst. They are damaged enough to cause at least short-term interruption. Local rail connections to the port area pass within a few hundred yards of one of the refineries. This service incurs long-term disruption. An important consequence is the loss of rail connections to the massive food distribution center and produce terminal in the southeast corner of the city.

Road. Several major northeast-southwest highways are severed at the refineries and at bridge crossings over the Schuylkill River. While this poses serious problems for the immediate area, there are alternate routes through New Jersey and via the western suburbs of the city.

Ship. Except for the possible blockage of the channel by grounded or sunken ships in the narrow reach near the naval shipyard, ship traffic to and from the port experiences only short-term interruption.

Perhaps the most serious immediate and continuing problem is the destruction of many of Philadelphia's hospitals. Assuming a typical construction of multistory steel or reinforced concrete, hospitals would have a 50 percent probability of destruction at about 2.13 miles [3.4 km]. A detailed 1967 map indicates eight major hospitals within this area; all are destroyed or severely damaged. Another nine hospitals are located from 2 to 3 miles [3 to 4 km] from the refineries. Although most of the injured are in this area, their access to these hospitals is curtailed by rubble and fire. Thus, most of the seriously injured have to be taken to more distant hospitals in north and

northeast Philadelphia. These quickly become overtaxed.

Two important military facilities are located near the intended targets. The Defense Supply Agency complex is located within 0.5 miles [0.8 km] of one of the refineries and is completely destroyed. The U.S. Naval Shipyard is 1.0 to 1.8 miles [1.6 to 2.9 km] from the nearest target and suffers severe damage. The large drydocks in this shipyard are within a mile of the refinery.

Several educational, cultural, and historical facilities are in or near the area of heavy destruction. These include Independence Hall, the University of Pennsylvania, Drexel Institute of Technology, Philadelphia Museum of Art, City Hall, the Convention Hall and Civic Center, Veterans Stadium, Kennedy Stadium, and the Spectrum.

Reaction: The First Week

During this period people are in a state of shock, with their lives disrupted and further drastic changes inevitable. Many have lost their homes and loved ones. Factories and offices in the target areas are destroyed, throwing people out of work. People face many immediate tasks: firefighting, caring for the injured, burying the dead, and search and rescue.

Fires at petroleum refineries, storage tanks, and petrochemical factories rage for hours or days, adding to the damage caused by blast. Some oil tanks rupture, and the oil leaks into rivers or harbors, where fires ignite and spread. Fires at refineries cannot be extinguished because of intense heat, local fallout, an inadequate supply of chemicals to use on petroleum fires, and roads blocked by rubble and evacuees. Petrochemical plants, already damaged by the blasts, are further damaged by fire and leak toxic chemicals. Firestorms or conflagrations (see Chapter 3) are fed by thousands of tons of gasoline. Most plants are damaged beyond repair. Finally, with fires threatening to burn, poison, or asphyxiate people in shelters, rescue crews attach top priority to rescuing survivors.

Once it becomes clear that further attacks are unlikely, the undamaged areas of the country start to supply aid. However, available medical aid is totally inadequate to treat the burns this attack has caused. The radius in which third-degree burns occur (5.9 miles [9.6 km] for a 1 Mt weapon air burst) is far greater than for any other life-threatening injury, and huge fires have caused more burns. But, even in peacetime, the entire United States has facilities to treat only a few thousand burn cases adequately at any one time.

If the attack used ground bursts exclusively, it would cause fewer prompt fatalities (2.9 million instead of 5.0 million for the air burst case), but much fallout. Given the extensive fallout sheltering described above, about 312,000 people would still die of fallout. Fallout casualties, however, would depend strongly on wind directions. Would gulf coast fallout blow toward Atlanta, Miami, Cuba, or Venezuela? Would New Jersey fallout land on New York City on its way to sea? The problems of shelterees are discussed later in this chapter under "A Counterforce Attack Against the United States."

Beyond the physical damage, people begin to realize that a hidden assumption in their lives — that nuclear war could not occur — was dead wrong. Even people beyond target areas know immediately that secondary effects will irrevocably change their way of life, and survivors traveling to undamaged areas drive this point home. Most people will fear further attacks and seek protection by evacuating or seeking shelter. While recovery plans can be made and damage assessed, little reconstruction can occur with so many people dead, evacuated, or in shelters. The reaction period will not end until most people act as if they believe the war is over.

The Recovery Period

Once people believe the war is over, the nation faces the task of restoring the economy. The human consequences are severe, but most deaths occur within 30 days of the attack. Economic disruption and the economic recovery process last much longer.

Restoring an adequate supply of refined petroleum will take years. It is unlikely that any of the attacked refineries can be repaired, although enough infrastructure might survive to make it cost effective to clear and decontaminate the rubble and rebuild on the old sites. The attack has killed many people skilled in building or operating refineries. The attack has also destroyed many ports with special facilities for handling large quantities of crude oil and refined petroleum. The attack leaves the United States with about a third of its prewar refining capacity and with little of its prewar oil-importing capacity. This situation will persist until new refineries and ports can be built.

The survival of a third of the nation's refining capacity does not mean that everyone gets a third of the petroleum they got before the war. The government quickly imposes rationing. Critical industries and services have top priority — military forces, agriculture, railroads, police, firefighting, and so on. Heating oil can be supplied, but at austere levels. Uses of petroleum for which there are substitutes receive little or no petroleum. Railroads substitute for airlines, trucks, and buses on intercity routes; mass transit substitutes for private automobiles and taxis in local transportation.

The demise of the petroleum industry shatters the American economy, as the attack intended. A huge number of jobs depend on refined petroleum: manufacture, sales, repair, and insurance of cars, trucks, buses, aircraft, and ships; industries that make materials used in vehicle manufacture, such as steel, glass, rubber, aluminum, and plastics; highway construction; much of the vacation industry; petrochemicals, heating oil; some electric power generation; airlines and some railroads; agriculture; and so on. Thus, many workers are thrown out of work, and many industries forced to close.

The limited direct economic damage, already multiplied by thousands of secondary effects, is multiplied again by tertiary effects. Economic patterns that rest on the petroleum economy are disrupted. Much of the American way of life depends on automobiles — from fast-food restaurants and shopping malls to suburban housing construction and industries located on major highways, whose workers commute by car. The many people thrown out of work have less money to consume things made by others. Service industries of all kinds are especially hard hit.

Economic changes lead to social changes that have further economic consequences. Gasoline rationing at best will severely curtail use of private cars; mass transit is used to its capacity, which appears inadequate. Mass movement within and between cities begins to upset the demographics underlying taxes, schools, and city services. With many people out of work, demand for unemployment compensation begins to rise at the same time taxes are falling. The economic system on which production depends has been radically changed, although most workers and equipment have survived unscathed and economic recovery will eventually take place.

Production depends, however, not only on the use of physical resources, but also on a wide range of understandings between producers and consumers. These underpinnings have been destroyed by the attack just as surely as if they had been targeted. Prices are uncertain, and various kinds of barter (trading favors as well as goods) supplement the use of money. Credit and finance can not function normally in the absence of information about the markets for continuing production. Contracts have uncertain meaning. Many businesses go bankrupt as patterns of supply and demand change overnight. Courts are seriously overburdened with the task of trying to arbitrate the huge load of new claims. Corporations and individuals are reluctant to make commitments or investments.

Given this disruption, the effort to resume production requires grappling with some basic organizational questions. To which tasks should surviving resources be applied? How can people be put back to work? What mix of goods should they produce? Which industries should be expanded, and which curtailed? Which decisions should government make, and which can be left to the market?

This organizational task is unprecedented, but it can in principle be performed. During the mobilization for World Wars I and II, extensive government planning supplemented private enterprise, and key assets and key people from the private sector were borrowed by the government for the duration of the emergency. Following nuclear attack, certain tasks, such as caring for the injured, decontamination, high-priority reconstruction, and serving as an employer of last resort (to say nothing of meeting military requirements) will obviously be handled by the government. A major difficulty lies in planning and facilitating the transformation of the private sector. Manning unusable factories and service facilities with unemployed workers could easily create an economic situation analogous to that experienced in the United States from 1929 – 33.

Long-Term Effects

In post-attack society, people will live in different places, work at different jobs, and travel in different ways. They will buy different things and take different kinds of vacations. The nation will apply the lessons of the past to future policy by seeking to reduce its vulnerability to another attack. Energy conservation, where not required by regulations, will be encouraged by prices, taxes, and subsidies. Railroads and mass transit will supplant travel by cars and planes; rail and ships will substitute for planes and trucks in hauling freight. Automobile production will drop sharply and emphasize energy-efficient models; bicycles and motorcycles will be popular. New homes in the suburbs will be built closer together so that mass transit can serve them. Many houses will be better insulated; more will use solar energy as fuel costs soar.

Most farms should be able to obtain adequate supplies of petroleum and its derivatives. Agriculture uses only 4 or 5 percent of the nation's petroleum, and its products are necessary. Although gasoline and petrochemical-based fertilizers and pesticides will be much more expensive, they comprise only a small fraction of farm expenses and are essential for large-scale, efficient agriculture. Moreover, much fertilizer is made from natural gas rather than petroleum, so its price will not rise as dramatically as that of gasoline. As ever, petroleum-related cost increases will be passed on to the consumer. The character of agriculture could change, however.

In particular, the livestock industry might be sharply curtailed. At every stage, livestock raising, slaughter, and distribution require much more energy than do crops. For example, rapid transportation and extensive refrigeration are required. Because meat will become far more costly in relation to other foods, it will be a luxury. With the drop in livestock production, a major source of demand for corn, soybeans, and other fodder will decline, possibly slowing price increases for other farm products.

Although most refineries and oil importing facilities will be rebuilt, U.S. refining capacity after recovery will probably be less than pre-attack capacity. Increased prices for gasoline and heating oil will shift demand to other sources of energy, raising their prices and encouraging an acceleration of their development.

Patterns of industrial production will shift dramatically because of these changes, forcing massive shifts in demand for skills and resources. Many people and factories will suddenly discover that they are oriented to the production of things no longer in demand; it will take many years for the economy to adjust to the massive changes imposed by the attack.

The attack will affect public health; Chapter 6 discusses the long-term effects of sublethal levels of radiation. Petrochemical plants damaged by the attack will leak carcinogenic petrochemicals, but numbers of cancer cases from this source, the time of their appearance, and the duration of the threat cannot be predicted. To the extent that contamination or destruction of housing, and economic collapse, force people to live in substandard housing, illness will increase.

Not all changes, however, will be for the worse. Some new patterns of living will promote public health. There will be fewer auto, aircraft, and boating accidents. More people will walk or bicycle, increasing exercise. Reduced consumption of meat will reduce dietary fats, heart attacks, and strokes. At some point, government-imposed controls necessitated by the attack could be lifted because societal changes and market forces (price increases, alternative energy sources, residential patterns, and numbers and efficiency of cars) will achieve the goals of control without coercion. For

example, gasoline rationing, which was imposed immediately after the attack, might be lifted in stages as refining capacity is restored; subsidies to expand and support mass transit could level off or decline as revenues made it self-supporting.

Summary

The nation's adjustment to all these changes would be painful. The problems would be especially severe because of the speed of their onset. Many people say that the United States would be better off if it was less dependent on cars and petroleum. While changing to new patterns of living via nuclear attack would minimize the political problems of deciding to change, it would maximize the difficulties of transition. Problems would appear all at once, while any advantages of new patterns of living would come slowly.

A U.S. ATTACK ON SOVIET OIL REFINERIES

In this hypothetical case, the United States tries to inflict as much economic damage as possible on the Soviet Union by using 10 SNDVs. No effort is made either to maximize or minimize casualties. Petroleum refineries were selected as targets because of their small number, long construction time, and the severe economic consequences of a lack of refined petroleum.

The Soviet refining industry is at least as vulnerable as its U.S. counterpart, although the vulnerabilities differ slightly. The United States refines more petroleum than does the U.S.S.R., about 17.9 million barrels per day of crude (1978 figures) versus 11.0 million (1980 projection).[2] According to a 1977 source, the U.S.S.R. had 59 refineries, including at least 12 under construction, some of which are very large; the U.S. and its territories have at least 288.[3] All individual refineries in both nations are highly vulnerable to nuclear attacks. The U.S. attack destroys most of the Soviet refining capacity because the U.S.S.R. has few refineries; the Soviet attack destroys most of U.S. refining capacity because U.S. refineries are clustered.

The hypothetical U.S. attack targets 24 refineries and 34 petroleum storage sites. Because some major refineries are beyond range of Poseidon missiles, the United States uses 7 Poseidons with a total of sixty-four 40-kiloton (kt) RVs and 3 Minuteman IIIs with a total of nine 170-kt RVs. Because of the dispersal of Soviet refineries and limits of footprint size, each footprint had fewer refineries than available RVs. The additional RVs were first allocated 2 on 1 against large refineries; remaining RVs were targeted against petroleum storage complexes. As in the U.S. case, every weapon is assumed to detonate over its target and destroy it. It is also assumed that all weapons are air burst; the consequences of using ground bursts are noted where appropriate.

Immediate Effects: The First Hour

The attack destroys 73 percent of Soviet refining capacity and 16 percent of Soviet storage capacity, as shown in Table 10. Collateral economic damage could not be calculated, nor could collateral damage to a large Soviet city be assessed.

If all weapons are air burst, the attack kills 1,458,000 people, assuming everyone is in single-story buildings, and 836,000, assuming everyone is in multistory buildings. The latter assumption is closer to reality. If all weapons were ground burst, the attack would kill 1,019,000 peo-

ple, 722,000 promptly and 297,000 by fallout, assuming the worst case — everyone living in single-story buildings.

Estimated injuries from the attack are substantial. Under the single-story housing assumption, the air-burst attack produces 3.6 million injuries and a surface-burst attack about a million less. If in multistory buildings, the population suffers 3.8 million injured from an air-burst attack and 2.5 million for the surface burst. A protection factor of 5 was assumed against fallout from the surface bursts.

The attack kills fewer Russians than Americans. The differences in fatalities do not mean that the United States is necessarily more vulnerable than the Soviet Union; rather, the asymmetries occur from the design of the attack. Soviet refineries are farther from cities than are U.S. refineries, and U.S. weapons are smaller, so fewer Russians are within the lethal radii of U.S. weapons. Sensitivity of fatalities and injuries to distance from ground zero is shown in Table 11. Had either nation sought to kill people, it would have used different weapons and targeted them differently.

Reaction: The First Week

As in the United States, life for the surviving Soviet majority is totally disrupted. Many people are directly affected by the attack: the injured,

TABLE 10.   Summary of U.S. Attack on U.S.S.R.

Footprint number	Geographic area (approx. center)	EMT[a]	Percent national refining capacity	Percent national storage capacity	Air burst prompt fatalities (x 1,000) SS[b]	MS[c]
1	Moscow	1.20	10.5	2.1	62	41
2	Baku	0.96	9.8	1.5	224	152
3	Ishimbai	1.20	8.7	2.8	25	12
4	Polotsk	0.92	7.5	0.3	52	32
5	Kuibyshev	1.20	7.4	3.1	127	83
6	Angarsk	0.92	6.9	0.4	130	54
7	Grozny	0.96	6.7	1.6	56	37
8	Kirishi	0.92	6.2	0.3	493	230
9	Gorki	1.20	5.6	1.5	228	153
10	Perm	0.96	3.6	2.1	61	42
	Totals	10.44	72.9	15.7	1,458	836

[a]EMT = Equivalent megatons.
[b]SS = 100 percent of population in single-story buildings.
[c]MS = 100 percent of population in multistory buildings.

TABLE 11.   Approximate Distance of Various Effects From
Selected Nuclear Air Bursts

	Effect	Weapon yield		
		1 Mt	170 kt	40 kt
Overpressure (crushing)	Lethality—			
	Threshold	0.25	0.15	0.1
	Lung damage—			
	Threshold	2.1	1.1	0.7
	Severe	0.8	0.5	0.3
	Broken eardrums—			
	Threshold	3.5	2.0	1.2
	50%	1.0	0.6	0.4
Translation	Personnel in the open—1%	3.3	1.6	0.9
	Personnel near structures—			
	1%	3.8	1.9	1.0
	50%	2.1	1.0	0.6
Thermal	Third-degree burn—100%	5.2	2.6	1.5
	No burns—100%	8.7	4.8	2.8
	Flashblindness*	10	9	8
	Retinal burn*	25	23	20
Radiation	Lethal dose (1,000 rads)	0.9	0.8	0.7
	No immediate harm (100 rads)	1.2	1.1	1.0

*Daytime safe distance.

those with missing or injured relatives, the homeless, people affected by shortages. Accommodation to a future with a sharply reduced petroleum supply begins. Gasoline and other products are hoarded, by enterprises if not by individuals. Some less-important industries are probably closed to save fuel or to allow their workers to shift to the military, agriculture, and essential industry. Until it becomes clear that the war is over, millions of reservists are mobilized for military service, placing a heavy demand on the domestic economy to replace them. Because of the mobilization, working hours and production mix change dramatically overnight. Workers in essential industries might be on 12 hour shifts. Other workers who have not been drafted are pressed into service in essential industries and quite possibly moved to factories in distant areas. The speed and magnitude of disruption cause much psychological shock.

How does the Soviet Union cope with the damage? Although a greater percentage of its refining capacity is destroyed, it suffers fewer fatalities than the United States (1.0 to 1.5 million versus

3.2 to 5.0 million) and fewer injuries (2.5 to 3.8 million versus 3.9 to 4.9 million) because of the lower yield of U.S. weapons and the location of Soviet refineries away from cities. If all weapons were air burst at optimum height of burst, there would be negligible fallout in both countries; if all weapons were ground burst, the Soviet Union would receive far less fallout. Because the Soviets have built many widely dispersed, small dispensaries and first aid centers, rather than small numbers of modern, full-service hospitals concentrated in cities, more of these facilities survive than in the United States. In addition, many Russians have received first aid training, and people with injuries who are treated by paramedics, dispensaries, and first aid are probably better off than their untreated American counterparts; others are at least as bad off. Those who require treatment at major hospitals suffer because of the small number of beds in nearby modern hospitals and the inability of the Soviet transportation system to move them elsewhere. Like the United States, the U.S.S.R. cannot cope with large numbers of severe burn cases. Many victims of severe burns in both nations die for lack of adequate treatment.

The damage, emergency conditions, and risk of further attacks remind everyone of the horror the Soviets faced in World War II. The psychological trauma is exacerbated in the first week by anticipation of crisis economic conditions. In past crises the Soviet government has proved to be ruthless and efficient in moving people to parts of the country where labor was needed. Such action is likely in this crisis as well, along with cutbacks in food, consumer goods, housing construction and maintenance, and transportation. Regimentation is likely to increase. Life will be grim and remain so for years.

The Recovery Period

What course will Soviet recovery take? Economic viability will not be at issue, and the government can be expected to remain firmly in control because of the limited scale of this attack. Assuming no further attacks, most of the deaths will occur within 30 days. While the course of economic recovery cannot be predicted in detail, it is clear that:

- The attack will hurt. The recovery period is marked by shortage and sacrifice, with particular problems stemming from agricultural shortfalls.
- Nevertheless, the Soviet economy and political system survive, and probably do so with less drastic changes than the United States would experience.
- The asymmetries between the two nations are greater for this case than for a very large attack.

The political and economic structure of the U.S.S.R. appears able to cope with drastic emergencies such as this attack. While most economic assets are unscathed, resources need to be shifted rapidly to produce a different mix of outputs. The attack totally disrupts existing economic plans. The economic planning apparatus and government control methods in place will permit the government to shift plans and resources, but the speed with which such changes can be made is uncertain. To the extent that revisions in the economic plan are not made or are delayed, people and equipment will sit idle or produce according to less-efficient priorities, draining scarce resources from higher priority tasks and thereby hindering recovery. Workers will be shifted to different industries as plants close; some will be forced to move, share apartments with strangers, or work at new jobs (including manual labor in farms or factories).

Some insight into the economic consequences can be obtained by looking at four sectors of the Soviet economy — military, agriculture, transportation, and industry. Each has a strong claim on available petroleum, but their total demand far exceeds the supply.

The military has first call on fuel, especially if the war continues. It has adequate stocks to wage war for several weeks. However, unless this attack led to a decisive Soviet victory or to a major relaxation of tensions, the military would need refined petroleum to rebuild its stocks and carry out normal training.

Soviet agriculture is precarious even in peacetime because of its inefficiency. Agriculture engages about a third of the work force and consumes a third of Soviet gasoline and diesel fuel. U.S. agriculture, in contrast, uses 2.7 percent of the work force (in 1978) and a small fraction of U.S. refined petroleum.[4] The Soviet Union imports grain in most years. Nevertheless, the U.S.S.R. has maintained a large cattle industry at considerable expense to provide a consumer good that is much in demand. Farms use petroleum for tractors and trucks; petroleum and natural gas are feedstocks for fertilizer and pesticides. Agricultural use of petroleum is increasing. An example is the recent use of light aircraft to spread fertilizer; while this task could be done by tractors or by hand, it is more efficient to use aircraft.

Cutbacks in petroleum would magnify agricultural inefficiency. Even if the Soviet Union allocated all the petroleum it produced to agriculture, it could not produce enough to sustain agriculture's prewar consumption. Following the attack, the main concern of agriculture is planting, growing, or harvesting the year's crop. Sacrifices and substitutions will be required in other agricultural subsectors to meet this goal with available petroleum. The U.S.S.R. is likely to divert people from schools, factories, and (depending on the international situation) the military to work the fields, as it does in peacetime, but to a greater extent. The substitution of human labor for mechanical energy is a poor but perhaps unavoidable trade-off. The most obvious cutback is livestock. Meat is a luxury because livestock consume much food that could otherwise be used for human consumption, and cattle raising, slaughter, and distribution require much energy. After the attack, the Soviet Union may slaughter much of its livestock to free farmers, fields, trucks, and petroleum to produce crops. Russians might have a 3 month orgy of meat followed by two decades without.

Soviet transportation will be pinched. A few top leaders still have cars; other cars sit idle for years, monuments to the prewar standard of living. Air transportation is sharply curtailed, and Soviet supersonic transports are grounded. Truck transportation is curtailed, with trucks used almost exclusively for intracity transportation and hauling goods between railroads and loading docks. By elimination, the transportation burden falls to railroads because of their energy efficiency. Key trunklines are electrified and might obtain electricity from sources other than petroleum. The Soviets have stored a number of steam locomotives, which can be hauled out, refurbished, and put to use.

The tempo of industrial production will slow. Even now, the Soviets have barely enough energy and occasional shortages. Electric power will probably be cut back 10 to 15 percent, forcing some industries to close and reducing heat and light at other industries and homes. With transportation cut back, factories have to wait longer for inputs, lowering productivity.

Some less-essential industries, especially energy- or petroleum-intensive ones, may shut down. Plastics use petroleum derivatives as feedstocks. Aluminum production uses great amounts of energy, though some Soviet aluminum plants, such as the one at Bratsk in Siberia, use hydroelectric power. Truck production will

stop because of the lack of fuel for existing vehicles. The huge Kama River truck plant will be idled.

Construction consumes much petroleum, so it will be curtailed except for essential industries, hydroelectric powerplant construction, refining construction, and minimal housing for workers in those occupations.

These changes will disrupt workers' lives. Closing of some plants will idle many workers, forcing them to work in other industries; many will be moved long distances to other plants. Workers are not necessarily forced to work long hours. While some plants will operate around the clock, others may be closed or cut back to enable the energy they consume to be diverted. At the same time, however, workers may be diverted from closed to open plants, providing extra labor for factories that remain open extra time.

In sum, the reduction in the standard of living and the amount of disruption will probably be less than in the United States, but there might well be more hardship and misery. Russians will have less food, especially protein, than they did before the attack. American agriculture consumes so little petroleum, however, that its output could probably be maintained, although some variety might be sacrificed. There will be less heat in both nations, but winters are shorter and milder in the United States, and U.S. indoor temperatures in winter can be reduced 5° or 10°F without ill effect. Therefore, heating could probably not be cut as much in the U.S.S.R. as in the United States without jeopardizing health. Cars will be sacrificed at least temporarily in both nations. Soviet industries producing consumer goods will be cut back more sharply than their U.S. counterparts, and will regain productivity more slowly.

Long-Term Effects

Destroying 73 percent of refining capacity will force the Soviet economy to assume a crisis footing, curtailing choices and consumer goods, dropping the standard of living from austere to grim, and setting back Soviet economic progress by many years. Recovery might follow the post-

World War II pattern, with a slow but steady improvement in the quality of life. But recovery will be slow. The desire to reduce vulnerability to future attacks will undoubtedly divert resources from recovery to such tasks as building some underground refineries. While the United States can possibly recover in a way that uses less petroleum than it did before the war, this course is difficult for the U.S.S.R. because much of Soviet petroleum goes to necessities. Long-term health and genetic effects will be less than for the United States because of the smaller size of U.S. weapons and the location of Soviet refineries away from people. But the Soviet government might accept greater radiation exposure for people in order to speed production. This would increase the deleterious effects from radiation.

A COUNTERFORCE ATTACK ON THE UNITED STATES

The case of a Soviet attack on U.S. strategic forces has received extensive public attention in recent years, since some observers believe it the least irrational way of waging strategic warfare. For the purposes of this book, the military success of such an attack (i.e., how many U.S. forces would be destroyed) and the resulting U.S. responses are not important. It is sufficient to assume that such an attack is launched, and to examine the consequences for the civilian population, economy, and society. Small variations in the attack design (e.g., whether control centers as well as silos are targeted) are immaterial.

A question of particular interest is whether the attack would be delivered only against ICBM silos, or whether bomber bases and missile submarine bases would also be attacked. Some of the public discussion suggests that an attack on ICBM silos alone would cause much less civilian damage than a full-scale counterforce attack because the silos are more isolated from population centers than are bomber bases. Although an attack that included bomber bases and missile submarine bases would certainly cause more civilian damage than one that did not, the difference between an attack limited to silos (called a *counter-*

silo attack) and a comprehensive counterforce attack would be no greater than the difference made by other variables, such as the size of weapons used, the proportion of surface bursts, and the weather. Both cases are considered in this section; the countersilo attack is a subset of the counterforce attack. However, available data are too coarse to differentiate between the civilian effects of each attack.

Immediate Effects

The blast damage from a counterforce attack is concentrated on military installations. Attacks on submarine bases and bomber bases cause considerable blast damage to nearby populations and urban structures; attacks on silos cause relatively little civilian blast damage. Unlike ICBM silos, many bomber bases and fleet ballistic missile submarine support facilities are near cities. (See Figure 15.) For example, an attack on Griffiss Air Force Base, near Utica and Rome, N.Y., would expose nearly 200,000 people to prompt effects; attacking the submarine support facility near Charleston, S.C., would endanger more than 200,000 people; attacking Mather Air Force Base, near Sacramento, Calif., would endanger more than 600,000 people. The additional attacks would simultaneously reduce the number of people able to provide aid and increase the number of injured or evacuees requiring aid. These attacks would make it harder for the able to sustain those needing aid.

Countersilo attacks would probably detonate some weapons at or near the earth's surface to maximize the likelihood of destroying ICBM silos. Surface bursts produce intense fallout, causing most of the damage to the civilian population, economy, and society. The principal civilian impact of adding attacks on bomber and SSBN bases is a large increase in urban destruction.

Fallout begins to reach nearby populated areas in a few hours; it will reach many others in a few days. As fallout arrives, radiation levels rise sharply and rapidly. People must therefore take any protective actions — shelter or evacuation — before the fallout arrives. This prearrival period

FIGURE 15.   Counterforce Targets in the United States

● Operational SAC bomber bases
△ ICBM fields
■ SSBN support bases
☆ State capital

NOTE: No targets in 15 States; one target each in 11 States

is thus one of intense activity and confusion. How will people react? Training can help, but even trained people will fare poorly if they can not get to shelters or if shelters are unstocked. To what extent will people panic, seek other family members, or evacuate spontaneously, and what are the consequences of such actions?

The decision on whether to evacuate is complicated. Evacuation is reasonable for people endangered by blasts from further attacks, but evacuation is a poor strategy for people at risk from fallout alone. It is difficult or impossible to predict the safe areas and the hot spots, and a car in a traffic jam offers poor shelter indeed.

Shelter is in theory available to a majority of people, although the best available shelter might not be adequate in areas where the fallout proved

to be very intense. However, the practical difficulties of fallout sheltering may be very great. The time to seek shelter may be very limited. People will not know how long they have, and they will want to get their families together first. A shelter must have a sufficient protection factor. Fallout particles must be kept out of the shelter, which requires a ventilation system more complicated than an open window or door, and if people enter a shelter after fallout has fallen there must be some means of decontaminating them. Water is necessary; heat may be necessary depending on the time of year; sanitation is a problem. Finally, without radiation rate meters, people cannot tell how long they must remain in the shelter.

The time of day, the time of the year, and the degree of emergency preparations during the hours or days before the attack will all affect the number of deaths. Whatever the circumstances, the few hours after the attack see a frantic effort to seek shelter on the part of most of the American population. Then, in densities and locations determined by the attack parameters and the weather, the fallout descends. Many Americans are lucky enough to be in areas where the fallout level is low. Many others (between an estimated 2 million and 20 million) are caught without shelter, or with inadequate shelter, and die. Still others suffer from a degree of radiation that makes them sick, or at least lowers their life expectancy, but does not kill them immediately. The trials of living in fallout shelters are intensified by the fact that many people do not know in which category they and their families fall.

A comprehensive counterforce attack would impose a greater burden than a countersilo attack. Many more people would be injured by prompt effects, and people near bomber and SSBN bases would have only a few minutes warning in which to seek shelter. Cities in the blast areas—those near submarine or bomber bases—would be heavily damaged. A few cities, such as Charleston, S.C., and Little Rock, Ark., could suffer consequences similar to those discussed earlier for Detroit or Philadelphia; most would not. People in blast areas would face similar hazards—injuries from blast, direct nuclear radiation, and thermal radiation, and from such secondary effects as falling buildings and fires. As in other cases, rescue would be difficult, with streets blocked by rubble, water pressure gone, and emergency vehicles destroyed.

People in areas damaged by blast and in the path of fallout will be in greatest peril. Injuries, damage to prospective shelters, damage to transportation, and damage to utilities can make them highly vulnerable. Little Rock, the site of an ICBM base and a bomber base, would receive both blast damage from a pattern attack (designed to destroy bombers in flight) and intense fallout radiation from the attack on ICBMs.

People in areas neither damaged by blast nor threatened by fallout would still believe themselves to be in danger of blast or, at a minimum, fallout until it was clear that the attacks had

ended. To these people will fall the burdens of producing necessities and caring for the injured and evacuees. Yet people in these areas, believing themselves to be in danger, will feel compelled to seek shelter or, especially in unattacked cities, to evacuate spontaneously. These actions will reduce the flow of aid to damaged areas. Indeed, the economy will probably shut down until people are certain that the war has ended and most people can get back to work. Even if some people report to work, production will be difficult with many absentees. If production stops even for a week, the loss will be tremendous. But this counterforce attack will disrupt the economy less than a limited attack on oil refineries, because most productive resources will remain intact.

Human fatalities are the most important component of damage and the easiest to estimate. To estimate fatalities, the critical questions are which areas are damaged by blast, and to what extent? How much fallout is there and where is it deposited? These questions cannot be answered with great confidence.

The Office of Technology Assessment drew on several recent studies of counterforce attacks. These studies differed widely in their results, primarily because of differences in their assumptions. OTA felt it more useful to look at how these assumptions affect the results than to attempt to determine the "correct" assumptions. Consequently, a range of results is presented; if OTA had done a new study of this case the results would probably have fallen somewhere in this range.

The countersilo studies indicate that between 2 and 20 million Americans will die within the first 30 days after an attack on U.S. ICBM silos. The wide range of results stems from the extent of the uncertainties surrounding fallout. The key uncertainties are height of burst, weapon design, weather, terrain, and distance from the blasts.

Height of burst. If the fireball touches the ground, it vaporizes some dirt, irradiates it, and draws it up into the mushroom cloud. This material condenses to become fallout. The lower the height of burst, the more the fireball touches the ground, and the more fallout produced. An air burst in which none of the fireball touches the ground creates negligible fallout. Because ICBM silos are very hard, a surface burst offers the greatest probability of destroying the silo with one explosion; it also maximizes fallout. The probability of destroying an ICBM silo is increased if two warheads are targeted against it, but fallout will double if both are surface bursts.

Weapon design.   Some weapons derive more energy from fission (as opposed to fusion) than others; the more fission, the more fallout. The weapon yield also affects the amount of fallout; the higher the yield of a given explosion, the greater the fallout.

Weather.   The speed and direction of the wind at various altitudes determine the directions and distances of fallout deposits. They also influence fallout concentration. Winds typically vary with season. This variance is so great that it can affect casualties by a factor of three, as Figure 16 shows. The hourly and daily variation of winds also can affect casualties. In general, winds can not be accurately predicted even after an attack takes place, much less in advance. Raindrops collect fallout particles from the radioactive cloud, thereby creating areas of intense fallout where it is raining, and reducing fallout elsewhere. The same is true for snow.

Terrain.   Hills, buildings, and ground temperature gradients (such as those caused by highways and small lakes) affect the exact pattern of fallout, creating hot spots in some places and relatively uncontaminated spots nearby.

Distance.   Other things remaining constant, fallout decreases with distance from the explosion beyond roughly 50 miles [80 km].

As explained in Chapter 3, radiation from fallout in large doses causes death, in smaller doses causes illness, and in still smaller doses creates a probability of eventual illness or early death. As explained in Chapter 4, protection can be obtained when matter is placed between the fallout and people. In general, the more matter (the greater the mass) between a source of radiation and a person, the greater the protection and the higher the protection factor (PF). The adequacy of a given PF depends on the intensity of the fallout. For example, a PF of 20 (typical of a home basement with earth piled over windows and against

the walls) would reduce an outdoor radiation level of 60 rem per hour to an indoor level of 3 rem per hour. In this case, a person outdoors for 10 hours would almost certainly be killed by radiation, and a person in the basement shelter would have a good chance of survival. But if the outdoor level is not 60 rems per hour but 600 rems per hour, a PF of 20 is inadequate.

The studies mentioned previously made separate calculations for countersilo attacks and for counterforce attacks including bomber and missile submarine bases. Assuming that there is no pre-attack evacuation, calculated deaths range from a low of 2 million to a high of 22 million. The differences result primarily from variations in assumptions regarding fallout protection. The high figure assumes approximately the degree of protection that people receive in their daily peacetime lives (PF of 3), and the low figure assumes that immediately after the attack the entire population moves to fallout shelters with a PF of at least 25. A more reasonable assumption, that the fallout shelters which now exist are utilized by people living near them, yields 14 million dead. The same studies also assessed the effects of extensive pre-attack evacuation (crisis relocation), and found that it reduced the range of predicted deaths. However, the degree of fallout protection, both for those who evacuate and those who remain near home, is still the most important consideration.

Given the threat U.S. bombers pose to the Soviet Union, a Soviet preemptive counteforce attack on bomber bases would probably seek to destroy the aircraft and supporting facilities rather than crater the runways. To destroy airborne bombers launched on warning of attack, an attacker might detonate weapons in a spaced pattern over the base. Air-bursting these weapons rather than ground-bursting them could reduce the threat of fallout but increase casualties from blast and thermal effects. If the weapons were detonated much above the optimum height of burst for maximizing overpressure on the ground, fallout would be negligible and blast damage would be reduced. The attacks against missile submarine bases are much less complex. A single high-yield weapon with medium-to-good accuracy

FIGURE 16.   Expected Casualties as a Function of Typical Monthly Winds

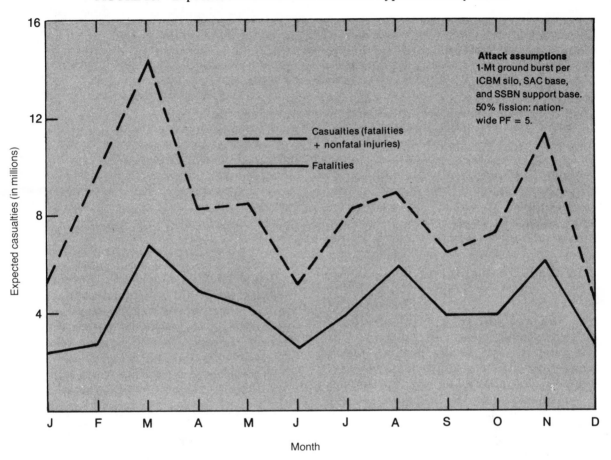

would destroy docks, piers, cranes, and other facilities — and nearby cities, factories, and people as well.

Accordingly, if the only difference between two attacks is that one attacks only ICBM silos and the other attacks bomber and missile submarine bases as well, the latter attack will kill more people. However, the variations in assumptions made about attack design, weather, and fallout protection obscure this clearcut result. Since these variations reflect genuine uncertainties, it is not possible to determine which fatality estimate is most probable. However, some of the extreme assumptions do appear implausible. One Defense Department study notes that its highest fatality figure assumed the use of Soviet weapons larger than those which U.S. intelligence estimates the Soviets possess. Very low fatality estimates assume abnormally low winds, an absence of surface bursts, or virtually perfect fallout protection. On balance, all that can be concluded is that "studies of hypothetical counterforce attacks show deaths ranging from 1 million to 20 million, depending on the assumptions used." However, the low end of this range (deaths below the 8 to 10 million level) requires optimistic assumptions, while the high end of the range is plausible only on the assumption that the attack is not preceded by a crisis period during which people are educated about fallout protection.

The data on injuries contained in these studies are quite limited; for the counterforce attacks, however, the results suggest that injuries would about equal fatalities.

The Contamination Period

For several days or weeks, radioactive contamination becomes so intense that people in fallout areas have to stay in shelters or evacuate. What might be called the "shelter period" begins at each location when fallout starts arriving and ends when people can leave their shelters long enough to do a day's work. The length varies from place to place; many places receive no fallout, and some hot spots are hazardous long after surrounding areas are safe. However, people can go outside for brief periods before an 8 hour day outside a shelter becomes safe, but can not live in houses with a low protection factor for weeks after an attack. After 2 or 3 months people can ignore the residual radiation, though it will be far higher than is considered "safe" in peacetime.

For the first 10 to 30 days, people in the intense fallout areas will have to remain in shelters most of the time. Brief excursions outside to obtain water or food, for example, will substantially reduce the effective protection factor. Life in a shelter is difficult at best. People will not know if the shelter offers a sufficient PF, or whether further attacks are imminent. The shelter might be dark, as power could be out, and the windows covered with dirt. Unless the shelter has a good air filtration system, the air will become clammy and smelly, and carbon dioxide concentration will increase. Supplies of food and water might or might not be adequate, depending on what people brought and how many people were in a shelter. Unless the shelter is specially stocked, medical supplies will probably be inadequate. This will be a severe problem in light of the unhealthy conditions in shelters. People who require special medicines will be in special danger unless they can obtain an adequate supply. While most people have radios to receive broadcasts, few have two-way radios to transmit. Although phones may still work, it will be difficult to obtain help because anyone in a contaminated area who leaves a shelter will be in jeopardy from radiation. In particular, medical care will probably be

unavailable because of the radiation risk of going to a hospital and the tremendous number of patients seeking help at the few hospitals that remain open.

Radiation sickness will present special problems. Exposures too low to cause acute radiation sickness nevertheless lower bodily resistance to infection. Resistance is also lowered by a deterioration in sanitation, prolonged exposure to heat or cold, lack of medical care, psychological shock, and inadequate food, water, and medicine. Hence, shelterees will be especially vulnerable to contagious diseases, ranging from colds and influenza to typhoid fever. There is a trend in the United States away from immunization; as a result, many will contract diseases they otherwise would not.

While many people will contract radiation sickness and live, it is very difficult for the non-medical person to determine whether an individual showing pronounced symptoms of radiation sickness has received a moderate, severe, or lethal dose. Moreover, acute psychological shock induces symptoms similar to radiation sickness, and vomiting—a symptom of both—is contagious in small spaces. Thus, someone who vomited would not know if he had received a moderate, severe, or lethal dose of radiation; had severe psychological shock; had vomited because of contagion; or had some other illness. This uncertainty, and nausea itself, would increase the tension in a shelter.

Some people will be better off than others: those in adequately equipped shelters of good PF; those who are neither very young, very old, nor ill; those who have received little or no radiation before entering the shelter; those in less-crowded shelters. Moderate outdoor temperature would be better than hot, and hot would be better than cold. People in snow zones in the winter, however, are more likely than others to have adequate provisions as a precaution against being stranded at home by snow. In addition, much depends on how shelterees use their time to prepare the shelter before fallout arrives.

Even if the winds are perverse, there will be substantial areas of the country that receive little or no fallout. In some cases (e.g., Oregon), no fallout would be expected unless the war continued after the counterforce attack; in other cases it will be several days before people in an uncontaminated area are certain that they are among the lucky ones. Once it becomes clear that a certain area has been spared, the people living there will step up their normal pace of activity. To the extent possible, help could be offered to the contaminated areas. Depending on circumstances, there may be large numbers of evacuees to care for. The major task, however, will be to keep the country going until the other survivors emerge from shelters. Intense but rather disorganized activity is likely, and essential production will probably occur.

Most productive resources survive unscathed, but shut down until the threat of attack has ended. Plants in fallout areas remain closed until radiation levels diminish, with the possible exception of such critical services as radio stations, water pumping facilities, and sewage disposal units. Some plants will operate as intensively as possible to meet the demands of the damaged areas and the injured, and to compensate for loss of production elsewhere. The burden imposed on the economy by the armed forces will depend on their internal cohesion and on the international situation.

Most economic damage occurs from lost production, but there are other losses as well. Fires burn unchallenged, and machinery suffers damage from being shut down in haste or not at all, or from being left outside unprotected. The major damage to the economy, however, results from deaths and long-lasting injuries to consumers and producers, and personal tragedies and other traumas that make people less able to work. The magnitude of economic loss will be proportional to the number of deaths.

The attack will cause considerable economic disruption in uncontaminated areas. Facilities there will need to produce a vastly different mix of goods and cope with the absence of goods that normally come from contaminated areas. Until people believe the war is over, it may prove difficult to organize production in the uncontaminated areas. Uncertainties about the legal and financial arrangements that support production (money, contracts, credit, etc.) may impede production. Some workers, fearing further attacks, will spontaneously evacuate. Public disorder could also impede production. Changes and uncertainties will cause some economic disruption; however, the greater effort put forth would probably more than compensate for it.

Recuperation

Economic viability will not be at issue following a counterforce attack. Because the attack seeks no economic damage, it is far less likely than a deliberate strike on economic targets to create any bottlenecks that will greatly hinder recovery. The nation should be able to restore production and maintain self-sufficiency. Such an attack will cause enormous economic loss, but the nation's capacity for growth will at worst be only slightly impaired. The major task will be ending disruption and disorganization and putting the pieces back together rather than rebuilding the economy. Most likely these tasks would be accomplished by a mixture of individual, local, state, and federal initiatives, with federal intervention a last resort.

The main problem areas will be in agriculture, decontamination, public health, and economic disorganization.

Agriculture. The attack can be expected to destroy only a tiny fraction of farmland with blast and fire. Of much greater significance, fallout will contaminate a substantial fraction of cropland because many ICBMs are in or near the Great Plains. Other cropland will escape with little or no fallout. Only a small fraction of the livestock in nearby fallout areas will be adequately protected. Fallout will affect agriculture in two ways—by killing livestock and crops and by preventing farmers from working in the fields.

The damage from fallout contamination of crops depends on the time of year. Most crops take up relatively little fallout, and external irradiation does not contaminate them. Moreover, it is easy enough to remove fallout particles from food. However, the vulnerability of crops to fallout varies significantly with the type of crop and the stage of its growth. For example, yields of various crops can be reduced 50 percent by the following doses, in roentgens (R): peas, less than 1,000 R; rye, 1,000 to 2,000 R; wheat, corn, cucumbers, 2,000 to 4,000 R; cotton, melons, 6,000 to 8,000 R; soybeans, beets, 8,000 to 12,000 R; rice, strawberries, 12,000 to 16,000 R; and squash, 16,000 to 24,000 R. Young plants are most vulnerable to radiation, while those near maturity are least vulnerable.

Knowledge about radiation effects on crops is limited. Much more is known about gamma radiation effects on crops than about beta radiation. Since fallout emits both types, and since beta doses to plants could be from 1 to 20 times the gamma dose, this is a major uncertainty.

Although fallout will prevent farmers from working in fields for a time, fallout does decay, and weathering further reduces its effects on people. A year after the attack, fallout will no longer be of consequence to farmworkers in most areas. How soon after the attack they can begin work depends on the amount of fallout deposited on a field.

The overall effects will thus depend significantly on time of year. An attack between October and January will have little effect, because fallout will have decayed enough by planting time to permit farmers to work the fields and to avoid serious damage to crops. Radiation on fields can be substantially reduced by plowing the fallout under or by scraping off the top layer of dirt. An attack in February or March will delay planting, reducing crop yields or making it necessary to shift to crops that mature more quickly. An attack between April and June could kill the entire crop. An attack in July or August could have little effect if the plants are undamaged by radiation. But the resulting crop should be safe for human consumption in an emergency. An attack during or just before the harvest could result in the loss of the whole crop, not by damaging the plants, but by preventing farmers from harvesting.

Fallout is more damaging to livestock than to plants. Animals are only slightly more resistant to radiation than are people; for sheep, cattle, and pigs in barns, where they are protected from direct contact by ingestion of fallout, a dose of 400, 500, and 600 R, respectively, will kill half these

animals. The median lethal dose is considerably lower for animals in pastures, where they can eat fallout along with grass. Poultry are considered more resistant; a dose of 850 R will kill half the poultry in a barn. Many animals in heavy fallout areas will probably be killed, because farmers generally have no fallout shelters for animals. Moreover, depending on the damage the attack wreaks on human food crops, it might be necessary to use animal feed as human food. Consequently, it could take many years to rebuild the national livestock supply, and until then meat would be a scarce luxury.

Decontamination. Cities, farms, and factories in contaminated areas will require decontamination in order to reopen for human use. Decontamination involves moving fallout to areas where it can do less harm. It can be done with bulldozers, street sweepers, fire hoses, and brooms. It does, however, require people to place themselves in danger of added contamination. Will enough people be willing to run these risks? Training is required for people to know which doses are tolerable and which are not. Such training will make people more willing to face these risks, but will enough people receive this training?

Public health. Health standards will have to be lowered following the attack. In peacetime, standards are often set cautiously; when acceptable exposure risk is unknown, it is preferable to err on the side of safety. Following the attack, that option will not be available. Fields will be farmed while low-level radioactivity persists. The risks, quite unacceptable in peacetime, will be preferable to starvation. Moreover, how applicable will our knowledge be for setting standards for the entire population after an attack? Could enough instruments be made available to enable everyone to know what dose they were receiving? And what role will politics play in setting standards when "acceptable risk" rather than "negligible risk" is at issue? Society will be running greater risks without knowing just how great the risks are. There will be a consequent increase in low-level radiation sickness, cancers, and genetic damage.

Economic disorganization. Once people are confident that the war has ended, money will retain its value, and so will property in uncontaminated areas. But the marketplace that organizes the American economy will be severely disrupted by abrupt shifts in demand, abrupt changes in supply, and questions about the validity of contracts involving people or things in contaminated areas. In addition, a major question will develop over how to share the losses from the attack in an equitable way. Then, too, demands for military allocations will probably increase, placing greater burdens on the diminished productive capacity.

Long-Term Effects

The main long-term damage is caused by countersilo strikes, which create the great bulk of fallout even if bomber and missile submarine bases are also attacked. Radiation has long-term health consequences, such as cancers, other illnesses, genetic damage, and death that blast does not. Similarly, ecological damage is caused mainly by countersilo attacks; this topic is dealt with in Chapter 6.

In the long run, the economy will recover, although it will be decades before the people killed will be "replaced" in either a demographic or an economic sense. There will undoubtedly be permanent shifts in demand. For example, there might be little market for houses without basements or fallout shelters, and the supply of some goods, notably meat, might be scarce for some time.

An imponderable is the psychological impact. The United States has never suffered the loss of millions of people, and it is unlikely that the survivors would simply take it in stride. The suffering experienced by the South in the decade after 1860 provides the nearest analogy, and a case can be made that these effects took a century to wear off.

A COUNTERFORCE ATTACK ON THE SOVIET UNION

As in the previous Soviet counterforce attack on the United States, the main threat to the civil-

ian population, economy, and society comes from fallout, while the damage done to the strategic forces is beyond the scope of this book. Here, too, OTA drew on the executive branch calculations, and the uncertainties are very great.

Each of the variables that affect the damage to the United States from a counterforce attack will also affect the damage to the Soviet Union. There is an additional source of uncertainty: U.S. missiles mostly carry smaller warheads than their Soviet counterparts, but U.S. bombers carry weapons with very high yields (see Appendix). Ground bursts of bomber-carried weapons (which are especially likely in an attack on Soviet bomber bases) will create tremendous amounts of fallout.

The First Day

As in the case of a counterforce attack on the United States, sheltering is preferable to evacuation, provided there are no subsequent attacks. Depending on the time of year, the Soviets might have more difficulty than the United States in improvising fallout protection (both frozen earth and mud will create problems). On the other hand, Soviet preparations for such sheltering in peacetime are more extensive than their U.S. counterparts.

In several calculations of fatalities resulting from counterforce attacks, variations in the assumptions produce a range of estimates. Most studies assume a Soviet first strike and a U.S. retaliatory strike. As a result, estimates of Soviet fatalities are lower than for a U.S. counterforce first strike, partly because the United States would have fewer ICBMs available for a second strike, and partly because the Soviets are more likely to take precautionary civil defense measures before a Soviet first strike than before a U.S. first strike. The studies only consider fatalities in the 30 days following the attack; they ignore later deaths resulting from relatively less intense radiation or the effects of economic disruption.

For both counterforce and countersilo attacks, with an in-place Soviet population, the fatality estimates are very similar: for the former, from less than 1 to 5 percent of the population; for the latter, from less than 1 to 4 percent. The low estimates result from using smaller weapons air burst, while the high estimates result from using larger weapons ground burst. A comprehensive counterforce attack can logically be expected to kill more people than the countersilo attack. However, other factors have a greater influence on numbers of fatalities. A full counterforce attack in which the United States deliberately tried to minimize Soviet fatalities by using small weapons air burst, in which winds were favorable, and in which the Soviets had tactical or strategic warning, would kill far fewer people than a countersilo-only attack in which the United States used one large weapon ground burst against each ICBM silo.

An unpublished Arms Control and Disarmament Agency (ACDA) analysis highlights the importance of sheltering and attack characteristics for fatalities from a U.S. countersilo attack. One estimate is that, with the urban population 90-percent sheltered and the rural population given a PF of 6, Soviet fatalities would range from 3.7 to 13.5 million, depending on attack parameters. With a degraded shelter posture (urban population 10-percent sheltered and rural population given a PF of 6), fatality estimates for the same set of attacks range from 6.0 to 27.7 million.

If bomber bases (or airfields with long runways) are attacked, tactical warning can be of great importance to people living nearby. In an area near each base (roughly, the area more than 1 mile [2 km] but less than 10 miles [16 km] from a surface burst), people who are sheltered at the moment of the blast will have a much greater chance of survival than those who are unsheltered. Soviet civil defense plans presume that civilians in such high-threat areas will receive some warning, but its extent cannot be predicted.

The Shelter Period

Many millions of Soviet citizens live in areas that will receive substantial fallout from such an attack. Those far enough away from the explosions to be safe from blast damage will have some time (from 30 minutes to more than a day) to shelter themselves from fallout, but evacuation from high-fallout areas after the attack will probably not be feasible. The Soviet civil defense program gives attention to blast shelters rather than fallout shelters in urban areas (see Chapter 4), and while such blast shelters will offer good protection against fallout, some of them may not be habitable for the necessary number of days or weeks protection is required.

The sheltering process will be much more tightly organized than in the United States. The Soviet government has extensive civil defensive plans, and Soviet citizens will expect the government to tell them what to do. Although efficient and timely action by the authorities will be very effective, Soviet citizens may receive fatal radiation doses while waiting for instructions or following mixed-up instructions. In any event, some hours after the attack a large number of people in contaminated areas will be in fallout shelters, others will be receiving dangerous doses of radiation, and those outside the fallout areas will be congratulating themselves on their good luck and hoping that no further attacks take place.

Will Soviet shelterees be better off than their American counterparts? They have several advantages. They are more accustomed to crowding and austerity than Americans, so will probably suffer less "shelter shock." They will be more accustomed to following government orders, so to the extent that orders are correct and correctly implemented, they will be more evenly distributed among shelters. Training in first aid and civil defense, which is widespread in the Soviet Union, improves people's ability to survive in shelters. If the U.S. attack uses low-yield warheads, fallout will be less widespread and less intense.

Soviet shelterees face some problems that Americans would not. They will be more vulnerable than Americans to an attack in winter. The Soviet economy has less "fat," so other things being equal, Soviet citizens could bring less food and supplies into shelters than Americans.

Public health is a major uncertainty. To the extent that shelters are well stocked, provided with adequate medications and safe ventilation, have necessary sanitary facilities, are warm and uncrowded, and have some people with first aid knowledge, health will be less of a problem. If Soviet citizens receive less fallout than Americans, they will be less weakened by radiation sickness and more resistant to disease. If conditions are austere but reasonably healthy, public health in shelters will be mainly a matter of isolating ill people and practicing preventive medicine for the others. Doctors are unnecessary for most of these tasks; people trained in first aid, especially if they have some access (by phone or radio) to doctors, can perform most tasks. To be sure, some people will die from lack of treatment, but the number will be relatively small if preventive care works. However, isolating the ill will not be easy. Many people will probably be moderately ill (from flu, etc.) when they enter a shelter, and radiation will make the others more susceptible to contagion. The Soviet government may send medical teams to contaminated areas, especially to shelters containing workers with key skills. The Soviet Army has built tanks and some other military vehicles with protection against fallout, and has trained its soldiers for operations in contaminated areas. In addition, as in the United States, military helicopters can ferry people and supplies into contaminated areas with limited exposure to crews. Use of such resources will obviously help the shelterees, but military tasks may take priority.

People in expedient shelters, if they can be built, will face worse health problems, despite the legendary ability of Russians to endure hardships. Presumably these shelters will have inadequate supplies, heat, air filtration, sanitary facilities, waterproofing, and so on. Placing people in a cold, damp hole in the ground for 2 weeks with little food and makeshift toilets would make many people sick even in peacetime. How well could such problems be overcome in war?

Soviet civil defense presents a large question mark. Some believe that the Soviets have massive food stockpiles, meticulous plans detailing where each person should go, ample shelter spaces, subways and buildings convertible to shelters, and other provisions that would be valuable in the shelter period. Others say these claims are vastly overstated and confuse speculation about a plan with its existence and the existence

of a plan with its operational effectiveness (see Chapter 4). If Soviet civil defense works well, it will save many lives; if it doesn't, Soviet shelterees will face conditions at least as hazardous as their American counterparts.

As in the United States, agricultural losses will depend on the time of the year the attack came and on the precise patterns of fallout. In general, Soviet agriculture appears more vulnerable because it borders on inadequacy even in peacetime. Even relatively minor damage would hurt, and major crop losses could be catastrophic. On the other hand, for this very reason the Soviets will know how to cope with agricultural shortages. Surviving production and stockpiles (the extent of Soviet food stockpiles is a matter of controversy, apart from the fact that they are lowest just before each harvest) will probably be used efficiently.

The economy outside the contaminated areas will continue to function. There will be more than enough industrial facilities in uncontaminated areas to keep necessary production going. The key task facing government planners will be using available workers and resources to best advantage. How fast could planners generate new economic plans detailed enough for that task? Because the Soviet economy operates closer to the margin than the United States economy, the Soviets can tolerate less loss of production. Superproduction will be required, with key factories working all the time. This will lead to suspending production of many consumer goods. The government will probably begin decontamination earlier and take more risks with radiation exposure than would the United States. These actions will be aided by the government's control of the economy, particularly by its keeping work groups together in shelters and host areas.

The Recuperation Period

As in the United States, economic viability will not be threatened by such a counterforce attack. The key questions are how appropriate Soviet emergency plans are and how rapidly planning mistakes can be corrected. Major shifts, and the inefficiencies that accompany them, are inevitable. To what extent can planning minimize them? Can a planned economy do better under the circumstances than a market economy? The Soviet Union's long experience with central planning means that the changes will involve details within the existing system rather than a change from one economic system to another.

In the U.S.S.R., as in the United States, the crop loss caused by the attack will depend on season, fallout deposition, and which crops are hit by fallout. Similarly, the amount of food reserves will vary with the season. The immediate problem for agriculture will be supplying enough food for the cities. Presumably, the government will try to meet this goal by tightening controls rather than giving farmers more capitalistic incentives. For a counterforce attack, with little physical damage, controls would probably work.

It is questionable whether there will be enough labor available for agriculture. Depending on the situation, millions of men may be mobilized into the army. On the other hand, the Soviets have well-established procedures for getting military personnel, factory workers, and others to help with harvests. Moreover, following a nuclear attack, some workers in nonessential industries will be out of work and could be sent to farms. The overall Soviet exposure to radiation will be high because of the large number of farmers (perhaps 35 to 40 percent of the Soviet work force is in agriculture, compared to 2 or 3 percent in the United States), the fallout contaminating some farmland, and acceptance of more exposure to radiation.

If a year's crop is lost, will there be austerity, short rations, or starvation? How much surplus food is there? In particular, is there enough to maintain a livestock industry, or will meat be seen as a nonessential consumer good and feed grains diverted for human use?

As in the United States, the attack will create many burdens for the Soviet economy. Military expenditures will probably increase. People injured by the attack will need care, and fewer people will be alive or well enough to care for them. Major changes in the economy will cause inefficiencies. Lowered public health standards will

increase early production at the expense of later health burdens.

The Soviet Union will not face certain problems faced by a market economy. The legal and financial devices supporting production — money, credit, contracts, and ownership of productive resources — are far less important there than in the United States. Instead, Soviet production is guided by a central plan. Contingency planning has reportedly been done for postwar recuperation. Such contingency plans (or the peacetime plan if there are no applicable contingency plans) will have to be adjusted to take account of the actual availability of surviving workers and economic assets. Doubtless such adjustments will be made, though not without some waste and inefficiency.

All things considered, a counterforce attack of this nature could be somewhat less damaging than World War II was to the Soviet Union, and Soviet recovery from that conflict was complete. However, the Soviets were victorious in 1945 and were able to draw on resources from Eastern Europe. Much will depend on whether, in the aftermath of this counterforce attack, the Soviet people are pleased or appalled at the results of the war and on the relative power and attitudes of the Soviets' neighbors.

A MASSIVE ATTACK ON THE UNITED STATES

A massive attack is normally associated with all-out nuclear war. The attack uses thousands of warheads to attack urban-industrial targets, strategic targets, and other military targets. The number of deaths and the damage and destruction inflicted on the U.S. society and economy by the sheer magnitude of such an attack will severely test whether the United States can ever recover its former position as an organized, industrial, powerful country.

The Office of Technology Assessment wanted to examine purely retaliatory strikes for both sides, but all available studies involved Soviet first strikes and U.S. retaliation. However, the differences between a Soviet first strike and a retaliatory strike do not appear to be appreciably large in terms of damage to the civilian structure. Like the United States, the Soviets have a secure second-strike force in their submarine-launched ballistic missiles (SLBMs) and probably target most of them against the softer urban-industrial targets. Moreover, a U.S. first strike probably would not destroy the bulk of Soviet ICBMs before they could be launched in retaliation.

The effects of a large Soviet attack against the United States are devastating. The most immediate effects are the loss of millions of human lives, accompanied by similar incomprehensible levels of injuries, and the physical destruction of a high percentage of U.S. economic and industrial capacity. The full range of effects resulting from several thousand warheads — most having yields of a megaton or greater — impacting on or near U.S. cities can only be discussed in terms of uncertainty and speculation. The studies that address this level of attack report a wide range of fatality levels reflecting various assumptions about the size of the attack, the protective posture of the population, and the proportion of air burst to ground burst weapons.

A DOD 1977 study estimated that 155 to 165 million Americans would be killed by this attack if no civil defense measures were taken and all weapons were ground burst. In 1978, the DCPA looked at a similar attack where only half the weapons were ground burst; this assumption reduced the fatality estimate to 122 million. ACDA's analysis of a similar case estimated that 105 to 131 million would die.

If people made use of existing shelters near their homes, DOD's 155 to 165 million fatality estimate would be reduced to 110 to 145 million, and the DCPA's 122 million fatalities to 100 million. ACDA's comparable fatality estimate drops to 76 to 85 million. Again the ACDA figure is lower because it assumes air bursts for about 60 percent of the incoming weapons. Finally, if urban populations are evacuated from high-risk areas, the estimated prompt fatality levels are substantially reduced. The DOD study shows fatalities of 40 to 55 million; DCPA shows a very large drop to 20 million from the 100 million level. The primary reason for the 2-to-1 differen-

tial is the degree of protection from fallout assumed for the evacuated population. However, the effectiveness of evacuation measures in saving lives is still a matter of heated debate, and these reduced casualty figures must be viewed with extreme caution.

In summary, U.S. fatality estimates range from a high of 155 to 165 million to a low of 20 to 55 million. None of the analyses attempted to estimate injuries with the same precision used in estimated fatalities. However, DCPA did provide injury estimates ranging from 12 to 33 million, depending on circumstances. And remember that all of these fatality figures are for the first 30 days following the attack; they do not account for subsequent deaths among the injured or from economic disruption and deprivation.

The First Few Hours

The devastation caused by a single 1 Mt weapon over Detroit, and two similar weapons near Philadelphia, was described earlier. In this attack the same destruction takes place in 30 or so other major cities. Many cities with smaller populations are also destroyed. The effects on U.S. society are catastrophic.

The majority or urban deaths are blast induced — victims of collapsing buildings, flying debris, being blown into objects. Except for aiding the injured, the next most pressing task for most survivors is getting reliable information about what has occurred, what is taking place, and what is expected. In a disaster, timely and relevant information is critical to avoiding panic, helpful in organizing and directing productive recovery efforts, and therapeutic to the overall psychological and physical well-being of those involved. Presumably, the civil preparedness functions are operating well enough to meet some of this need.

Rescuing and treating the injured will be carried out against nearly insurmountable odds. Fire and rescue vehicles left intact will find it impossible to move about in any direction. Fires will be raging, water mains will be flooding, powerlines will be down, bridges will be gone, freeway overpasses will be collapsed, and debris will be everywhere. People will be buried alive, and without proper equipment capable of lifting heavy loads, the injured will be unreachable and will not survive. The ones that rescuers can reach will be faced with the unavailability of treatment facilities. Hospitals and clinics in downtown areas will probably be destroyed along with most of their medical supplies. Doctors, nurses, and technicians needed to staff makeshift treatment centers will be among the casualties. The entire area of holocaust will be further numbed by either the real or imagined danger of fallout. People will not know whether to evacuate their damaged city or seek shelter from fallout in local areas and hope there will be no new attacks. No doubt some of both will actually occur.

If this situation were an isolated incident or even part of a small number of destroyed cities in an otherwise healthy United States, outside help would certainly be available. But if 250 U.S. cities are struck and damaged to similar levels, one must ask, "Who will be able to help?" Smaller towns are limited in the amount of assistance they can provide their metropolitan neighbors. There would probably be no strong urge to buck a tide of evacuation to reach a place that most of the natives are trying to leave. Also, smaller cities and towns will have to cope with the anticipated arrival of fallout and refugees. Thus, in an attack of this magnitude, there will probably be no substantial outside assistance for the targeted areas until prospective helpers are convinced that the attack is over, and that fallout intensity has reached safe levels. Neither of these conditions is likely to be met in the first few hours.

The First Few Days

Survivors will continue to be faced with the decision of whether to evacuate or seek shelter locally during this interval. The competence and credibility of any remaining authority will be under continuous question. Will survivors be told the facts, or what is best for them to know? And who decides? Deaths will climb due to untreated injuries, sickness, shock, and poor judgement. Many people will evacuate simply to escape the

reality of the environment. For those staying, it probably means the beginning of an extended period of shelter survival. Ideally, shelters must protect from radiation while meeting the minimums of comfort, subsistence, and personal hygiene. Convincing people to remain in shelters until radiation levels are safely low will be difficult, but probably no more so than convincing them that it is safe to leave on the basis of a radiation-rate meter reading. There will be unanswerable quesitons on long-term effects.

Sheltering survivors in the populous Boston to Norfolk corridor will present unprecedented problems. Almost one-fifth of the U.S. population lives in this small, 150 by 550 mile [250 by 900 km] area. Aside from the threat of destruction from direct attack, these populations are in the path of fallout from attacks on missile silos and many industrial targets in the Pittsburgh, St. Louis, and Duluth triangle. Depending on the high altitude winds, the fallout from the Midwest will begin arriving 12 to 30 hours after the attack.

When fallout radiation first becomes intense, only a fraction of the surviving urban population will be in adequate fallout shelters. Those that are sheltered will face a variety of problems:

- making do with existing stocks of food, water, and other necessities or else minimizing exposure while leaving the shelter for supplies;
- dealing with problems of sanitation, which will not only create health hazards but also exacerbate the social tensions of crowds of frightened people in a small space;
- dealing with additional people wanting to enter the shelter, who would not only want to share scarce supplies but might bring contamination in with them;
- dealing with disease, which would be exacerbated not only by the effects of radiation but by psychosomatic factors;
- judging when it is safe to venture out.

Boredom will gradually replace panic, but will be no easier to cope with. Those with inadequate shelters or no shelters at all will die in large num-

A part of Hiroshima after the atomic blast

bers, either from lethal doses of radiation or from a combination of other hazards and weakness induced by radiation sickness.

The conditions cited above are generally more applicable to urbanites who are trying to survive. The problems of rural survivors are somewhat different; some are simpler—others more complex. With enough warning, people living in rural areas could readily fabricate adequate fallout shelters. However, it might be more difficult for a rural shelteree to have current and accurate information regarding fallout intensity and location.

The farm family is less likely to suffer traumatic exposure to death and destruction; consequently, it will probably be better prepared psychologically to spend the required time in a shelter.

Outdoor activity in or near major cities that are struck will probably be limited to emergency crews attempting to control fires or rescue the injured. Crews will wear protective clothing, but it will be necessary for any one crew member to severely limit total work hours so as not to risk dangerous accumulations of radiation. Areas not threatened by fallout could begin more deliberate fire control and rescue operations. The survival of a national facility to identify weapons impact points and predict fallout patterns is doubtful.

The extent of death and destruction to the nation would still be unknown. For the most part, the agencies responsible for assembling such information will not be functioning. This task must wait until the numbing effect of the attack wears off, and the government can once again begin to function, however precariously.

The Shelter Period

After the initial shock period, the problem of sheltering large masses of people will be compounded as the shelter time extends. Survival will remain the key concern. People will experience or witness radiation death and sickness for the first time. Many previously untreated injuries will require medical attention, if permanent damage or death to the individual is to be avoided. Stockpiles of medical, food, and water supplies are sure to become items of utmost concern. Whether some people can safely venture outside the shelter for short periods to forage for uncontaminated supplies will depend on fallout intensity—and the availability of reliable means to measure it.

This period will continue to be marked more by inactivity than activity. Many areas will be freed from the fallout threat either by rain, shifting winds, or distance from detonations. But economic activity will not resume immediately. Workers will remain concerned about their immediate families and may not want to risk leaving them. Information and instruction may not be forthcoming; if it is, it may be confusing, misleading, and of little use. Uncertainty and frustration will plague survivors, and even the smallest tasks will require efforts far out of proportion to their difficulty. Many will interpret this as symptomatic of radiation effects and become further confused and depressed. The overall psychological effects will probably worsen until they become a major concern and perhaps as incapacitating as physical injuries.

Deaths occurring within the first 30 days of an attack are categorized as prompt fatalities. This duration is a computation standard and is the basis for most fatality estimates. However, deaths from burns, injuries, and radiation sickness can be expected to continue far beyond this particular interval.

The Recuperation Period

The likelihood and form of economic recovery depends both on the physical survival of enough people and resources to sustain recovery and on whether these survivors can adequately organize themselves.

Physical survival of some people is quite probable, and even a population of a few million can sustain a reasonably modern economy under favorable circumstances. The survivors will not be a cross-section of prewar America, since people who live in rural areas will be more likely to survive than the inhabitants of cities and suburbs. The surviving population will lack some key industrial and technical skills; on the other hand, rural people and those urban people who survive are generally hardier than the average American.

Although the absolute level of surviving stocks of materials and products will seem low by prewar standards, a much smaller population will be using these stocks. Apart from medicines, which tend to have a short shelf life and are manufactured exclusively in urban areas, there will probably not be any essential commodity in desperately short supply at first. A lack of medicines will accentuate the smallness and hardiness of the surviving population.

Restoring production will be far more difficult than finding interim stockpiles. Production in the United States is extremely complex, involving many intermediate stages. New patterns of production that do not rely on destroyed facilities will have to be established.

The productive facilities that physically survive (undamaged or repairable with available supplies and skills) might not be adequate to sustain recovery. In some cases, scavenging among the ruins could provide adequate "raw materials" where natural resources are no longer accessible with surviving technology.

The most serious problems will be organizational. Industrial society depends on the division of labor, and the division of labor depends on certain governmental functions. Physical security comes first — people are reluctant to leave home to go to work without some assurance that their homes will not be looted. While some law and order can probably be maintained in localities where a fairly dense population survives, highways might become quite unsafe, which would reduce trade over substantial distances. The second requirement is some form of payment for work. Barter is notoriously inefficient. Payment by fiat (for example, those who work get government ration cards) is also inefficient and requires a government stronger than a postwar United States is likely to inherit. A strong government might evolve, but most surviving citizens will be reluctant to support a dictatorship by whatever name. The best solution is a viable monetary system, but it will not be easy to establish. Regions or localities might develop their own monies, with "foreign" trade among regions.

Surviving resources might not be used very efficiently. The surviving government will probably not be capable of surveying its surviving assets, especially since people will fear that acknowledgement of a surviving stock will invite its confiscation. To make use of surviving factories, workers will have to live nearby, and they might be unwilling to do so in the absence of minimally adequate housing for their families. Ownership of some assets will be hopelessly confused, thereby diminishing the incentives for investment or even temporary repairs.

The United States might break up into several regional entities. If these come into conflict with each other, there will be further waste and destruction.

In effect, the country will enter a race, with economic viability as the prize. It might try to restore production to the point where consumption of stocks and the wearing out of surviving goods and tools is matched by new production. If this is achieved before stocks run out, then viability will be attained. Otherwise, consumption will sink to the level of new production and probably depress production further, creating a downward spiral. At some point this spiral would stop, but by then the United States might have returned to the economic equivalent of the Middle Ages.

An all-out attack will be equally devastating to the U.S. social structure. Heavy fatalities in the major urban areas will deprive the country of a high percentage of its top business executives, government officials, medical specialists, scientists, educators, and performers. There is no way to estimate the impact of such lasting losses on our society. In addition to the irreplaceable loss of genius and talent, the destruction of their associated institutions is still another complication that is overlooked by some recovery estimates. How does one calculate how long it will take to get over the loss of Wall Street, an MIT, a Mayo Clinic, and the Smithsonian?

The American way of life is characterized by private ownership of items representing substantial long-term investments (such as homes, businesses, and automobiles). Widespread loss of these individual assets could have a strong, lasting effect on our social structure. Similarly, the question will arise of whether individual right to ownership of surviving assets should remain unchanged in a post-attack environment. For example, the government might find it necessary to force persons having homes to house families who had lost theirs.

The family group will be particularly hard hit by the effects of general nuclear war. Deaths, severe injuries, forced separation, and loss of contact could place inordinate strains on the family structure.

Finally, major changes will occur in the societal structure as survivors attempt to adapt to a severe and depressing environment never before experienced. The loss of a hundred million people, mostly in the larger cities, could raise doubts about the advisability of rebuilding the cities. Why rebuild obvious targets for a nuclear Armageddon of the future? The surviving population could seek to alter its social and geopolitical structure in hopes of minimizing the effects of any future conflicts.

How well the U.S. political structure might fare in a large-scale nuclear attack depends on a number of uncertainties. First, with warning, national officials are presumed to evacuate to outlying shelter areas; state and local authorities will take similar precautions, but probably with less success, especially at the lower levels. The confidence and credibility of the system will be severely strained as relief and recovery programs are implemented. Changes in an already weakened structure are sure to take place as many normal practices and routines are set aside to facilitate recovery. Survivors may demand more immediate expressions of their likes, dislikes, and needs. Widespread dissatisfaction could result in a weakening of the federal process, leading to a new emphasis on local government.

A MASSIVE ATTACK ON THE SOVIET UNION

A massive U.S. retaliatory attack against the Soviet Union will destroy 70 to 80 percent of its economic worth. The attacking force consists primarily of U.S. strategic bombers and Poseidon/Polaris SLBMs, since most U.S. landbased ICBMs are assumed lost to a Soviet first strike. Bombers carry gravity bombs and shortrange attack missiles having yields of about 1 Mt and 200 kt, respectively. Poseidon SLBMs nominally carry up to 10 RVs of 40 kt each.

The attack strikes the full set of Soviet targets — strategic offensive forces, other military targets, economic targets, and cities. The population is struck, although killing people is not in itself an attack objective. The objectives are to cause as much industrial damage as possible and to make economic recovery as difficult as possible. These attacks might not be limited in time. Concentrations of evacuees are probably not struck, but industries that recover very quickly after the attack might be.

The immediate effects of the attack are death and injury to millions of Soviet citizens, plus the destruction of a large percentage of Soviet economic and industrial capacity. As with the all-out Soviet attack, there is a wide range of casualty estimates, with the main uncertainty being the extent and effectiveness of Soviet civil defense measures.

If the Soviet population remains in place, fatal-

ity estimates range from a high of 64 to 100 million (26 to 40 percent of the population) to a low of 50 to 80 million (20 to 32 percent). With evacuation, an ACDA study estimates that fatalities will be reduced to 23 to 34 million. It is difficult to judge whether these estimates are a high or low. Nevertheless, Soviet fatalities are clearly lower than the United States for both in-place and evacuated populations. The lower Soviet fatalities are again primarily due to major differences in the yields of the weapons detonating in each country, and to the greater proportion of Soviet population that lives in rural areas.

As to the cause of fatalities (blast, thermal radiation, and direct nuclear radiation versus fallout radiation), DCPA data suggest that, in massive attacks, fatalities are primarily due to prompt effects instead of fallout. Prompt effects account for at least 80 percent of the fatalities when economic targets or population are included in the attack. In attacks on targets near urban areas, those protected enough to survive the blast effects also have enough protection to survive the fallout. But those who do not have enough protection against fallout in urban areas near targets will not have enough protection against prompt effects and will be dead before the fallout has an effect.

Estimates of Soviet injuries were generally not included in the analyses studied. However, one study suggested that injuries might be roughly equal to fatalities under certain attack and exposure assumptions.

The First Few Hours

As Chapter 4 noted, Soviet civil defense can have substantial impact on the full range of effects. Fallout shelters, blast shelters, and industrial hardening can reduce the overall damage from nuclear attack. First aid and civil defense training can ameliorate health problems. Storing supplies in shelters lengthens shelter stay time. Thus, the issue is how well Soviet civil defense will in fact work. Many unknowns — numbers of shelters, size of food and medicine stockpiles, smaller amounts of surplus resources than the United States — preclude a detailed judgment. It seems safe to assume, however, that Soviet civil defense measures would be at least as effective as U.S. measures and probably more so.

Pre-attack preparations will influence total damage. Because a U.S. retaliatory attack is by definition preceded by a Soviet first strike, it seems logical that some evacuation will have occurred. However, there are reasons why evacuation might not take place. An evacuation could increase the risk of a U.S. first strike; a U.S. attack might be so close at hand that an evacuation could increase casualties; a prolonged evacuation might be such an economic disruption that it would be better to wait until war appeared certain; or war could occur unexpectedly through miscalculation. In any event, a Soviet decision to strike first will allow the Soviets to make preparations — distribute supplies, improve and stock shelters, increase production of essential goods, harvest grain, protect livestock, conduct civil defense training and harden industrial facilities. These actions will also make Soviet citizens more responsive to civil defense instructions, especially to a warning that an attack is underway. While these actions will be observed by the United States, they are more ambiguous than an evacuation; the United States could interpret them as safeguarding against an attack rather than preparing for one.

The effects of evacuation in reducing casualties could be diluted if the United States varies its attack strategy. Spreading the attack over a period of time could extend shelter periods, enhance economic disruption, and delay rescue and emergency operations.

The Soviet Union, despite its vast geographical size, is vulnerable to urban attack in many of the same ways as the United States. Although there has been extensive publicity on the reported dispersal of Soviet industry, indications are that population and industry are becoming more and more concentrated. Some industries located away from cities are so concentrated that they form new targets of their own. Hedrick Smith describes

the Kama River Truck Plant as an archetype of the gigantomania of Soviet planners, as a symbol of the Soviet faith that bigger means better and the Soviet determination to have the biggest at any cost.

Kama is the kind of massive crash project that appeals to Russians.... It emanates brute strength. In 1971, Soviet construction brigades started from scratch to build the world's largest truck plant in the open, rolling, windswept plains about 600 miles east of Moscow.... Kama was not just one factory but six, all huge.... The production complex, costing in the billions, occupies 23 square miles, an area larger than the entire island of Manhattan. At full capacity, Kama is slated to produce 150,000 heavy trucks and 250,000 diesel engines a year, dwarfing anything in Detroit or the German Ruhr.[5]

The attack could cause "derussification." The U.S.S.R. is a conglomeration of nationalities, of which Great Russians — who dominate politics, industry, and much else — comprise about 48 percent. Most Great Russians live in cities; so an attack will reduce their numbers and influence, with unforeseeable consequences.

Timing makes a critical difference in destruction. An attack at night will find people with their families and more dispersed; they will seek shelter in apartment buildings. A daytime attack will strike people at factories and offices; to the extent they leave to find family members, chaos will result as in the United States.

An attack in winter will expose more people to bitter cold and impede evacuation. An attack in spring or fall, when many roads are made impassable by mud, will hinder evacuation by motor vehicle. An attack near harvest time could result in the loss of an entire year's crop, thus leaving food reserves at a low point. This effect could be magnified if the United States attacked agricultural targets, such as storage silos, dams, and drainage facilities.

Even time of month can make a difference because of the Soviet practice of "storming." The Soviet factory month in practice divides into three periods: "sleeping," the first 10 days; "hot" work, the second 10; and "feverish" work, the third. This division occurs because the economic plan calls for a specified output from each plant by the end of the month, but the inputs needed often arrive only after the 15th or 20th day. Thus, perhaps 80 percent of a factory's output is produced in the last 10 or 15 days of the month. Hypothetically, an attack around the 15th or 20th would cause the loss of most of a month's production by destroying large inventories of partially completed goods.

On the other hand, the U.S.S.R. has several important strengths. Soviet cities are generally less flammable than U.S. cities because there are more large apartment buildings and fewer wood-frame houses. These buildings also provide better shelter, especially those with built-in shelters. People expect to follow instructions and are less likely to evacuate spontaneously. The Party apparatus will probably survive with a far lower casualty rate than the population at large because it is well distributed and because blast shelters have been constructed for Party members. The nation is larger, which in theory provides more land area over which people can relocate, but much of the area is mountain, desert, or arctic.

The First Few Days

Actions in this period greatly affect the number of casualties and the amount of economic damage. Obviously, much damage occurs in the first hour. But many people trapped in the rubble can be rescued; others will be seriously injured but could survive with medical care or first aid; still others will be able to seek shelter or evacuate. Some industries will be damaged but not destroyed. If small fires are extinguished, undamaged equipment hardened against blast, and exposed equipment protected from rust, more resources will be available for recovery. Likewise, farms could harvest crops, shelter livestock, and protect harvested crops in the few days before fallout deposition.

The issue is not what can be done but what will be done. Proper use of time — organization and prioritization to get the most important tasks done with the least wasted effort and resources — will be critical. The Soviet system offers a major advantage in this period. As noted in the counterforce attack, the government's role in this crisis will be more clearly defined, and its control over individual action and the economy will be much stronger than that of the U.S. government in a comparable situation. Its experience with central planning and a command economy is good preparation for the actions needed — decisions involving large shifts in behavior and resources, and the formulation and dissemination of directives that will be obeyed without argument. Such actions will save some people and industries and condemn others, but taking the time to make better decisions could easily condemn more. Evacuation will have to be ordered in this period, or else would-be evacuees will have to wait until radiation has reached safe levels. For cities damaged only slightly, evacuation will prove difficult but not impossible. With many rail yards and some key bridges out, it will be difficult to get trains to smaller cities. Destruction of petroleum refineries, some petroleum storage capacity (especially that located in rail marshalling yards that are attacked), and some electric power generators will further impede evacuation by train. Fallout patterns are difficult to predict, so it will be hard to select the best evacuation routes and relocation centers. An attack in winter would add other problems.

Survivors in Soviet cities will face the same severe problems as those in U.S. cities. Many will be injured, trapped in rubble, or irradiated with direct nuclear radiation. Many shelters will be destroyed or damaged. Power will be out, so water pressure will be too low for fighting fires. Rubble will impede rescue.

Undamaged areas, especially those not threatened by heavy fallout, face severe burdens. They will receive many evacuees in the first few days, send rescue teams and resources to devastated areas, and strive to produce as much as possible. Evacuees in undamaged areas will be pressed into work in fields and factories, and sheltered in public buildings or private homes. The performance of undamaged areas will largely determine the nation's ability to prosecute the war and to achieve economic viability. The government will, however, face a dilemma in how to use the resources of undamaged areas. It could maximize current production, leaving workers and resources vulnerable to further attack, or it could seek to protect workers and resources, thus reducing current production. Specific choices will depend on the likelihood of further attacks and the criticality of various products, but the dilemma will still be there.

An all-out attack will exacerbate the peacetime inefficiencies of Soviet industry. The government will have to quickly determine what needs to be produced and whether the necessary factories exist, but it will have far more difficulty correlating inputs and outputs and arranging for their transportation. It will have to assign people to jobs and arrange for transport, shelter, and care of workers. Many will be dead, sick, traumatized, or debilitated by radiation sickness. However, the government will probably be able to control the movement of people. In peacetime, it exercises strong control of mobility. The Soviet people are not in the habit of going anywhere without permission, and everyone's actions must be justified and accounted for. In wartime, the government will presumably tighten its control of transportation. Generally, people will have no shelter from fallout unless the government arranges their transportation and shelter. This control will help the Government maintain economic organization following attack.

The Shelter Period

By all reports, the Soviets are better prepared than Americans to spend long periods of time in shelters. The protective structures shown in their literature are well conceived and should afford good survivability. Life in shelters and evacuation areas will in some ways be similar to that described earlier. Actions taken before fallout deposition will affect casualties. Public health, number and quality of shelters, and amount of stockpiled food and medicine are uncertainties. Civil defense and first-aid training will reduce deaths, but to an unpredictable extent. People in uncontaminated areas will be best off, followed by those in fallout shelters in contaminated areas, those in secure fallout shelters in blast areas, and those in hasty shelters in contaminated areas.

One public health problem will be especially acute. Antibiotics, which are invaluable in fighting many diseases but have a short shelf life and cannot be frozen, are in short supply in the U.S.S.R. even in peacetime. Antibiotics are typically used to compensate for the drastic decrease in antibodies in radiation victims, because it takes the body a long time to rebuild its antibodies after large radiation doses. Because of the U.S.S.R.'s limited supply of antibiotics, many people are expected to die from disease.

In areas contaminated by fallout but undamaged by blast, shelter life will be less intolerable. Utilities might be working; buildings will be undamaged and will offer better shelter. People will be uninjured. There will be time to prepare and provision shelters. There will be less inclination to evacuate and less pressure to leave shelters prematurely.

Fallout deposition patterns will become clear in this period; they will largely determine the damage to agriculture and the industries that need to remain closed. Harvesting crops uncontaminated by fallout will be impeded by fuel shortages, but evacuees will be plentiful and could harvest crops by hand. Similarly, evacuees could work in surviving industries in uncontaminated areas.

The key issue that the government will face is successful organization. Production will be far below prewar levels. It will be some time before the government can take inventory, set priorities, arrange for inputs of workers, resources, and power, and transport the outputs. Most needs in this period will be met from inventory. The government will thus need to establish strict inventory controls; it may be necessary to ration food severely, as was done in Leningrad during World War II.

Organizational problems will be especially critical in light of the intense struggle for resources and the need to distribute them as widely as possible. The competition for petroleum discussed previously will be minimal compared to the competition here. The military, agriculture, industry, transportation, and life support systems will all have urgent claims on resources. Everything will be in short supply; there will be hundreds of bottlenecks instead of one. How can the government mediate among these claims? There will be far less margin for error than in peacetime, and a decision to use resources for one purpose will almost automatically preclude other courses of action. Economic viability will be threatened, and deaths will increase because of delays in achieving it.

What sacrifices will the government demand? Each critical sector will be asked to make some, and consumer goods will probably be sacrificed altogether. Public health will be sacrificed to some extent by starting production early in contaminated areas and by giving people contaminated food rather than nothing.

The government will probably be able to maintain control. Food rationing, control of transportation and shelters, and internal passports will help the government restart the economy. Its economic plans will be the only alternative to chaos, and people will expect to obey government demands even without controls. Many Party members will survive. Contenders for resources will struggle inside the government, but external threats, the specter of chaos, the urgency of decisions, and the recognized impossibility of obtaining every necessity will dampen any debate. All sectors will make sacrifices. The military, for example, might forego fuel-intensive training. In agriculture and industry, manual labor will substitute for machinery. People will use wood for fuel where possible; many will be cold. Coal-burning locomotives will probably be taken from storage. Productivity will decrease before it increases. The standard of living will be far lower, and some will die in this period and in the next. The question is—how many?

Production—and with it, standard of living and the number of people production could support—will fall before it rises. Industries will use inventories of supplies for production, then close until supply can be reestablished. Transportation will wind down as petroleum refining is cut off and petroleum supplies become exhausted or requisitioned by the military. People will be diverted from production by being sick or injured, caring for the sick or injured, or being drafted for military service. What production takes place will be far less efficient. Many workers will be debilitated by minor cases of radiation sickness, other illness, malnutrition, psychological shock, and so on. Many will be asked to do tasks for which they lack the training or the physical strength. Factories will be damaged or unable to obtain necessary parts, so industrial managers will have to substitute labor for capital or use shortcuts that reduce the quality of a product or the efficiency of a process.

The Recuperation Period

If recovery goes well, production will stabilize at a level that makes good use of surviving resources and recover from there. The government will increase its control over people and the economy, production of consumer goods will be delayed, many resources will flow to the military, and public health will be lower, but sacrifices will pay off. Soviet engineers and plant managers are reputedly skillful at improvising solutions to mechanical problems. Such skills, government organization and control, and brute force could overcome bottlenecks, expand capacity, and give people austere but adequate food, housing, medical care, and other necessities.

The recovery could go poorly, however. A great many people could require unavailable medical care and die. The harvest could be lost, and more would die. Starving people would find and eat grain to be planted next year, reducing that crop and causing others to starve. Transportation could collapse. This would prevent factories from obtaining inputs, make it impossible for their products to be distributed, and force them to close. Hardening might save key machine tools, but access to them could be blocked by tons of rubble or high radioactivity. The government might be unable to conduct a detailed resource inventory that could integrate these tools into the economy, or there might be no way of transporting them to a factory that could use them. A war or threat of war, from NATO, China, or both, might divert surviving industry and materials toward the war effort and away from the economy. The direction of the economy is unpredictable because there are too many unknowns. But should economic productivity fall precipitously, for whatever reason, the economy would support fewer people and more would die. A failure to achieve viability could cause as many Soviet deaths as the attack itself.

In summary, the effects of a massive nuclear attack against Soviet military and urban-industrial targets will remove that nation from a position of power and influence for at least the remainder of this century. Soviet fatalities, due to asymmetries in weapons yields and population densities, will be lower than those for the United States. However, there is no evidence that the Soviet economy and its supporting industry will be less severely damaged than their U.S. counterparts. Nor is there any evidence that the Soviets face a lower risk of finding themselves unable to rebuild an industrial society.

6

Long-Term Effects

Even the immediate effects of a nuclear attack would have a long-term impact. Structures and resources that would be destroyed in seconds or hours might not be rebuilt or replaced for years, or even decades. The millions who would die in seconds or weeks (from fallout radiation) would not be replaced in a demographic sense for several generations. Some significant political, social, and economic changes arising from the immediate post-attack disruption would probably be irreversible.

There are other effects, however, that are "long term" in the sense that they would probably not be noticed for some months, or even years, after the attack occurred. Such effects include long-term somatic and genetic damage from radiation, certain changes in the physical environment, and changes in the ecological system. These are effects that conventional weapons cannot produce.

The long-term effects of nuclear war are placed in three separate catagories:

- effects from low-level ionizing radiation, which are reasonably certain to take place and whose magnitude would depend on the scope of the attack;
- damage to the ozone layer in the atmosphere, which could injure human and animal health and possibly lead to changes in the Earth's climate;
- other incalculable effects that should not be ignored.

The effects of low-level ionizing radiation can be calculated, to some extent, on the basis of existing data and theory. At present, it is not known how to calculate possible damage to the ozone layer, but ongoing research into the chemistry of the upper atmosphere promises some insight into this problem.

LOW-LEVEL IONIZING RADIATION

A large body of scientific literature addresses the long-term effects of low levels of ionizing radiation. Over the years there has been an intensive study of the health of the survivors of Hiroshima and Nagasaki, and some of those exposed to radioactive fallout as a result of nuclear weapons testing. There has been considerable research into the question of how many radioactive particles of various kinds are produced by nuclear explosions. There are theories regarding the effects of ionizing radiation on the human body. But there are also formidable uncertainties. New information is coming to light regarding some of the effects of past weapons testing, and there are unresolved scientific controversies over such matters as whether a small dose of radiation does more damage to the human body if it is absorbed during a brief period of time than if it is absorbed over a longer period. There are pertinent questions whose answers are only known to within a factor of ten.

Previous chapters have examined the effects of very intense ionizing radiation: 1,000 rems will almost certainly be lethal if absorbed within a matter of days; 450 rems will kill 50 percent of a healthy adult population, and a slightly higher percentage of the young, the old, and those without adequate medical care; 250 rems will cause acute radiation sickness, from which "recovery" is probable; lower doses may lower the body's resistance to infectious diseases of various kinds. Because of the rate at which fallout radiation decays, doses of 250 to 1,000 rems are likely to be received only during the first 30 days after an attack if they are received at all. The preceding chapter includes estimates of the numbers of people who might die from radiation effects during the first 30 days after various kinds of nuclear attack.

However, doses of ionizing radiation that are too small or too slowly accumulated to produce prompt death or radiation sickness can nevertheless have harmful effects in the long run. These effects are best discussed statistically, for it appears that if a large population is exposed to a small dose of radiation, some will suffer harmful effects while others will not. The larger the dose, the greater the percentage of the population that is harmed, and the greater the risk to any one individual.

There are a number of ways in which a nuclear attack would lead to radiation exposures that, although too low to cause death within the first 30 days, nevertheless pose an appreciable long-term hazard. Prompt radiation from the nuclear explosions could inflict sublethal doses on some survivors, especially if the weapons are small. Most of the radiation absorbed by survivors of the Hiroshima and Nagasaki attacks was direct radiation. A substantial number of U.S. weapons have yields in the tens of kilotons, and might inflict radiation on people far enough away from the explosion to survive the blast effects. Few Soviet weapons are of such low yields, and the blasts of their high-yield weapons are expected to kill those within radiation range. A terrorist weapon would almost certainly inflict direct radiation on survivors. There is particular uncertainty regarding the effects on humans of low levels of neutron radiation.

Local fallout will inflict small doses of radiation on people who are on the fringes of "fallout zones," or on people who are in fallout shelters in zones of heavier fallout. Even the best fallout shelters attenuate fallout rather than block it completely. The whole theory of fallout shelters is to insure that people who would otherwise receive a lethal dose will instead receive a sublethal dose. However, this sublethal dose will still produce harmful long-term effects for some percentage of those exposed.

After a period of time, local fallout radiation levels decay to the point where the area would be considered "safe," and survivors in fallout shelters would emerge. Nevertheless, low levels of radiation would persist for some time—indeed, they have persisted for years at some nuclear weapons test sites. The question of safety here is a relative one. By peacetime standards, many such areas would be considered unsafe, because living in them would expose a population to a significant risk of long-term hazards such as cancer and genetic damage. However, in the aftermath of a nuclear attack, there may be few habitable areas that do not have a low but measurable level of radiation, and the survivors would simply have to accept the hazards.

Some fallout is deposited in the troposphere, and brought down to earth (largely by rain) over a period of weeks. Such global fallout reaches areas quite far from the blast. While the doses inflicted would be relatively small, they would add to the risk.

Other fallout is deposited in the stratosphere. Gravity pulls it back to earth over a period of years. Consequently, only very long-lived radioactive isotopes pose a significant hazard here. If the attacks are confined to the territory of the United States, the Soviet Union, Europe, and China, then stratospheric fallout will be confined mostly to the Northern Hemisphere, and the region between 30° and 60° north latitude will receive most of it.

In quantifying the radiation dose received by individuals, radiation from external and internal (ingested) sources must be differentiated. External radiation passes through the skin. Ingested

TABLE 12.   Assumed Effects of Radiation Exposures

Effect	Number per million person-rems[a]
Somatic effects†	
Cancer deaths (DEF = 1)*...............	194.3[b][c]
Cancer deaths (DEF = 0.2)	38.9[d]
Thyroid cancers	131.4[e]
Thyroid nodules	197.4[e]
Genetic effects†	
Abortions due to chromosomal damage........	21-210[f]
Other genetic effects	66-660[f]

†These effects are in addition to those expected from natural or background causes.
*DEF = Dose effectiveness factor.
[a] This assumes that total exposure is governing—that is, that 1 rem each to a million people produce the same effects as 10 rems each to 100,000 people.
[b] This figure is modified from values presented in table VI, 9-4 of the Nuclear Regulatory Commission Reactor Safety Study (WASH 1400). The rationale for the modification was that although the latent period for cancer induction used by WASH 1400 was deemed appropriate, there is insufficient evidence that the plateau periods are limited to 30 years. Using the latent periods in WASH 1400 and the remaining lifespan as the plateau period along with the population age distribution, the cancer risk coefficients in the WASH 1400 study were converted to those in this table.
[c] See table 12 for the sources of these cancer deaths.
[d] Arrived at by multiplying the DEF = 1 figure by 0.2.
[e] Taken from table VI, 9-8 of the WASH 1400 report.
[f] These figures were derived from tables VI, 9-11 and VI, 9-12 of the WASH 1400 report. The range is based on a range of possible doubling dose from 20 to 200 rems, as suggested by the BEIR report (Washington, D.C.: National Academy of Sciences, 1972), p. 53.

radioactivity causes damage when particular radioactive isotopes are concentrated in specific organs. For example, radioactive iodine (I 131), which may enter the body through breathing, eating, and drinking, is concentrated in the thyroid, and radioactive strontium (Sr 89 and Sr 90) is concentrated in bone.

An OTA contractor performed a series of calculations to estimate the magnitude of the long-term health hazards that would be created by the long-term, low-level radiation that each of the OTA cases might produce. The basic method used was to calculate the total amount of radiation that all survivors of each hypothetical nuclear attack might absorb during the 40 years following the attack, and then calculate the numbers of adverse health effects that this much radiation could be expected to produce. Tables 12 and 13 present the risk factors used for these calculations.

The difficulties in such a procedure are formidable, and precise results are impossible to obtain. Following are major uncertainties (exclud-

TABLE 13. Assumed Sources of Cancer Deaths[a]

Cancer type	Cancer deaths per million organ-rems
Leukemia	45.4
Lung	35.5
Digestive tract	27.1
Bone	11
Others	75.3

[a]See footnotes a and b to table 12.

ing those in previous discussions about the size and nature of the attack, and the distribution of the population) that result in such a wide range of answers:

- How much of the population actually benefits from what degree of fallout sheltering?
- How many people die in the immediate aftermath of the attack?
- Does radiation that is part of a low exposure or a very slow exposure do as much damage per rem absorbed as radiation received as part of a high and rapid exposure?
- Is there a threshold dose below which radiation exposure does no harm at all?
- How does one deal with the age distribution of the population at the time of the attack, since susceptibility to cancer and other diseases from causes other than radiation varies with age?
- How great are the genetic effects from a given level of radiation?

There is still substantial debate about some of these questions. For example, one theory holds that, given time, the body can repair the damage done by radiation — that the same dose spread over years does less damage than it would if received within a few days. Another theory claims that radiation damages the body in ways that are essentially irreparable. The OTA study examined both alternatives — which accounts for some of the range in the final results. It also assumed no threshold dose, so that if one really exists, the results presented here are somewhat exaggerated. Finally, the genetic disorders resulting from

a given dose are difficult to estimate. One source estimates that anywhere from 20 to 200 rems could double the number of mutations occurring in a population in the years after attack. And it is even more difficult to predict how these mutations would manifest themselves in future generations.

The results of these calculations are summarized in Table 14. Although the actual results of a nuclear war would probably be some distance from either extreme, one can conclude that:

- Cancer deaths in the millions could be expected during the 40 years following a large nuclear attack, even if that attack avoided targets in population centers. These millions of deaths would, however, be far less than the immediate deaths caused by a large attack on a full range of targets.
- A large nuclear war could cause deaths in the low millions outside the combatant countries, although this would represent only a modest increase in the peacetime cancer death rate.
- These estimates might be far too conservative if an attacker deliberately tried to create very high radiation levels.

Just as the OTA report was going to press, the results of the National Academy of Sciences (NAS) Committee on the Biological Effects of Ionizing Radiations ("BEIR II") became available. In general, the new report suggests a slightly narrower range of uncertainty than the OTA calculations, but generally confirms their assumptions. OTA used assumptions of cancer deaths per million person-rems, which appear to be about 10 percent higher at the high end of the range and about 40 percent lower at the low end of the range than the findings of the new BEIR report. OTA calculated genetic effects on the basis of a doubling dose of 20 to 200 rems, compared with a range of 50 to 250 rems suggested by the new BEIR report, which may mean that the OTA estimates are too high at the high end of the range. The new BEIR report also notes that the incidence of radiation-induced cancer would be higher for women than for men.

TABLE 14.   Long-Term Radiation Effects from Nuclear Attacks[a]

A. Air Bursts

Estimated worldwide[b] effects from 1-Mt air burst over a city (OTA Case 1):

Somatic effects

Cancer deaths..............................	200 - 2,000
Thyroid cancers	about 700
Thyroid nodules	about 1,000

Genetic effects

Abortions due to chromosomal damage	100 - 1,000
Other genetic effects	350 - 3,500

Estimated worldwide[b] effects from an attack using 78 air bursts of 1 Mt each (OTA Case 2 attack on the United States) are 78 times as great, that is:

Somatic effects

Cancer deaths..............................	16,000 - 160,000
Thyroid cancers	about 55,000
Thyroid nodules	about 78,000

Genetic effects

Abortions due to chromosomal damage	8,000 - 80,000
Other genetic effects	27,000 - 270,000

Estimated total[c] effects from an attack using 72 air bursts of 40 kt each (OTA Case 2 attack on U.S.S.R.):

Somatic effects

Cancer deaths..............................	6,000 - 60,000
Thyroid cancers	about 50,000
Thyroid nodules	about 80,000

Genetic effects

Abortions due to chromosomal damage	2,500 - 25,000
Other genetic effects	5,000 - 50,000

B. Limited Surface Bursts

Estimated total[c] effects of an attack on U.S. oil refineries using surface bursts, with fallout sheltering treated parametrically:

Somatic effects	PF* = 5	PF* = 10	PF* = 40
Cancer deaths ..	2,000,000-5,500,000	1,000,000-3,000,000	300,000-1,000,000
Thyroid cancers .	about 2,000,000	about 1,000,000	about 300,000
Thryoid nodules .	about 2,500,000	about 1,500,000	about 500,000
Genetic effects			
Abortions due to chromosomal damage .	250,000-2,500,000	150,000-1,500,000	50,000-500,000
Other genetic effects ..	900,000-9,000,000	500,000-5,000,000	150,000-1,500,000

Estimated effects outside the United States from this attack:

Somatic effects

Cancer deaths..............................	8,000 - 80,000
Thyroid cancers	about 30,000
Thyroid nodules	about 50,000

Genetic effects

Abortions due to chromosomal damage	4,000 - 40,000
Other genetic effects	13,000 - 130,000

C. Counterforce Attacks (Mixed air and surface bursts—Case 3)

Estimated total[c] effects of an attack on U.S. ICBM silos, using one air burst and one surface burst (each 1 Mt) against 1,054 silos. A case in which bomber and submarine bases are also attacked with air bursts gives similar results. Fallout sheltering is treated parametrically:

Somatic effects	PF = 5	PF = 10	PF = 40
Cancer deaths ..	1,000,000-6,000,000	700,000-5,000,000	500,000-4,500,000
Thyroid cancers .	about 2,000,000	about 2,000,000	about 1,500,000

Continued

Somatic effects	PF = 5	PF = 10	PF = 40
Thyroid nodules .	about 3,000,000	about 3,000,000	about 2,500,000
Genetic effects			
Abortions due to chromosomal damage .	300,000-3,000,000	250,000-2,500,000	200,000-2,000,000
Other genetic effects ..	900,000-9,000,000	750,000-7,500,000	650,000-6,500,000

Estimated effects outside the United States from this attack:

Somatic effects

Cancer deaths..............................	400,000 - 3,800,000
Thyroid cancers	about 1,400,000
Thyroid nodules	about 2,000,000

Genetic effects

Abortions due to chromosomal damage	170,000 - 1,700,000
Other genetic effects	600,000 - 6,000,000

Estimated total[c] effects of an attack on Soviet ICBM silos, using one air burst and one surface burst (each 100 kt) against 1,477 silos. The overwhelming bulk of deaths are from "worldwide" (between 30° and 60° north latitude) fallout, and hence fallout sheltering in the Soviet Union makes little difference:

Somatic effects

Cancer deaths..............................	300,000 - 3,300,000
Thyroid cancers	about 2,500,000
Thyroid nodules	about 3,600,000

Genetic effects

Abortions due to chromosomal damage	120,000 - 2,500,000
Other genetic effects	400,000 - 4,000,000

D. Comprehensive Attacks (Case 4)

Estimated effects inside the United States of an attack on military and economic targets in the United States consisting of 3,325 weapons with a total yield of 6,500 Mt. A mixture of air bursts and surface bursts was assumed, and the ranges include variations in fallout protection available:

Somatic effects

Cancer deaths..............................	1,000,000 - 5,500,000
Thyroid cancers	1,000,000 - 2,000,000
Thyroid nodules	1,500,000 - 2,500,000

Genetic effects

Abortions due to chromosomal damage	150,000 - 6,000,000
Other genetic effects	400,000 - 9,000,000

Estimated effects outside the United States:

Somatic effects

Cancer deaths	900,000 - 9,000,000
Thyroid cancers	about 3,200,000
Thyroid nodules	about 4,500,000

Genetic effects

Abortions due to chromosomal damage	500,000 - 5,000,000
Other genetic effects........................	1,500,000 - 15,000,000

Estimated total[c] effects of an attack on military and economic targets in the Soviet Union consisting of 5,660 weapons with a total yield of 1,300 Mt. A mixture of air bursts and surface bursts was assumed, and the ranges include variations in fallout protection:

Somatic effects

Cancer deaths	1,200,000 - 9,300,000
Thyroid cancers	about 5,500,000
Thyroid nodules	7,700,000 - 8,400,000

Genetic effects

Abortions due to chromosomal damage	320,000 - 8,000,000
Other genetic effects........................	1,000,000 - 12,500,000

*PF = Protection factor.   [a]Assumptions and sources are those used for tables 12 and 13.   [b]Most worldwide fallout would be in the Northern Hemisphere, and it would be concentrated between 30° and 60° N Latitude.   [c]Includes worldwide totals (note b above), but effects are greater in the target country than elsewhere.

EFFECTS ON THE OZONE LAYER

Large nuclear explosions will inject a variety of particles into the upper atmosphere. In recent years, considerable attention has focused on the possibility that the injection of a substantial quantity of nitrogen oxide into the stratosphere by a large number of high-yield nuclear weapons might cause a depletion or thinning of the ozone layer. Such a depletion might produce changes in the Earth's climate. It would also permit more ultraviolet radiation from the Sun to penetrate the atmosphere and reach the Earth's surface, where it could produce dangerous burns, additional skin cancers, and a variety of potentially dangerous ecological effects.

In 1975, a report by the National Academy of Sciences (discussed more fully below) called this a serious danger, estimating that a 30- to 70-percent reduction in the ozone layer was a possibility. Since that time, however, there have been new findings and changes that have a bearing on the risk of ozone depletion. Further research into the chemistry of the upper atmosphere has modified the model calculations used in 1975. The results of past nuclear tests do not, however, provide data adequate for the complete validation of any model. There are also indications that the chemistry concerned is much more complex than was formerly believed. The current state of knowledge is roughly this: injections of nitrogen oxides could deplete the ozone layer if they occur at very high altitudes (80,000 ft [24 km] and upwards), which would result from very high-yield explosions (i.e., substantially more than 1 Mt) in large numbers (1,000 or more) or possibly from high-altitude explosions. Finally, the development of MIRVs has reduced the number of very high-yield warheads in the arsenals of the superpowers by replacing those warheads with multiple weapons of lower yield.

These changes by no means demonstrate that ozone depletion is impossible, and even slight depletion could cause an increase in the incidence of skin cancer. This is an area where research continues, and further findings are expected.[1]

INCALCULABLE EFFECTS

In 1975, the National Academy of Sciences published a report, *Long-Term Worldwide Effects of Multiple Nuclear-Weapons Detonations*, which addressed the question of whether a large-scale nuclear war would be likely to produce significant, irreversible effects on the world environment. This document may be summarized as follows:

- It is possible that a large nuclear war would have irreversible adverse effects on the environment and the ecological system.
- In particular, it would not require very large changes to greatly diminish the production of food. It would be difficult to adapt to such changes in view of the likelihood that much of the world's expertise in agricultural technology might perish in the war.

Leaves and new shoots started to appear on this chestnut tree two months after the explosion in Nagasaki, Japan.

- The physical and biological processes involved are not understood well enough to say just how such irreversible damage would take place.

Therefore, the NAS report could not estimate the probability or the magnitude of such damage. With the exception of the discussion of possible damage to the ozone layer, where new findings have come to light since 1975, these conclusions still hold.

There are at least two other kinds of hazards whose magnitude cannot be calculated. The radiation derived from a nuclear war would certainly cause mutations in surviving plants and animals, and some of these mutations might change the ecosystem in unpredictable ways. Furthermore, there is a possibility of major changes in human behavior as a result of the unprecedented trauma. Science fiction writers have speculated, for example, that in the aftermath of a nuclear war, the survivors would place the blame on "science" or on "scientists," and through a combination of lynching and book-burning eliminate scientific knowledge altogether. There are cases in history and archaeology of high civilizations that simply stopped functioning (though people survived biologically) after some shattering experience.

CONCLUSIONS

Calculations of long-term radiation hazards, with all their uncertainties, permit only rough conclusions:

- There would still be a substantial number of radiation deaths and illnesses among those lucky enough to escape a lethal dose during the first month after the attack.
- The number of deaths would be very large by peacetime standards, and the hazards much greater than those considered tolerable today.
- The number of deaths would be rather small compared to the number of deaths resulting from the immediate effects of the attack—millions compared to tens or hundreds of millions.

In contrast, the incalculable effects of damage to the Earth's ecological system might be on the same order of magnitude as the immediate effects of an attack.

Appendix: U.S. and Soviet Strategic Forces

The strategic forces assumed to be available for an early to mid-1980s conflict between the United States and the Soviet Union are derived from open-source estimates of weapons characteristics and force levels. Generally, the forces are assumed to be within SALT II established limits and assume the completion of ongoing intercontinental ballistic missile (ICBM) modernization programs of both superpowers. For the United States this means that yield and accuracy improvements for the Minuteman III force are carried out. On the Soviet side, it means completing the deployment of their fourth-generation ICBMs, the SS-17, SS-18, and SS-19.

A recent study conducted by the Congressional Budget Office, entitled *Counterforce Issues for the U.S. Strategic Nuclear Forces*, provided Table A1, which shows Soviet forces and their capabilities for the early to mid-1980s. Western estimates differ as to the exact attributes and ca-

TABLE A1. Estimated Soviet Strategic Nuclear Forces, 1985

Launcher	Number[a]	Warheads per launcher[b]	Total warheads	Yield in megatons[c]	Total megatons	Equivalent megatons
SS-11	330	1	330	1.5	495	432
SS-17	200	4	800	0.6	480	560
SS-18	308	8	2,464	1.5	3,696	3,228
SS-19	500	6	3,000	0.8	2,400	2,580
SS-16	60	1	60	1.0	60	60
Total ICBMs	1,398		6,654		7,131	6,860
SS-N-6. } SS-N-8. }	600	1	600	1.0	600	600
SS-N-17. } SS-N-18. }	300	3	900	0.2	180	306
Total SLBMs	900		1,500		780	906
Bear	100	1	100	20	2,000	740
Bison	40	1	40	5	200	116
(Backfire)	(250)	(2)	(500)	(0.2)	(100)	(170)
Total bombers	140 (390)		140 (640)		2,200 (2,300)	856 (1,026)
Grand total	2,438 (2,688)		8,294 (8,794)		10,111 (10,211)	8,622 (8,792)

SOURCE: *Counterforce Issues for the U.S. Strategic Nuclear Forces*, Congressional Budget Office, January 1978.

TABLE A2.　Estimated U.S. Strategic Nuclear Forces, 1985

Launcher	Number	Warheads per launcher	(Mid-1980's force)			Equivalent megatons
			Total warheads	Yield in megatons	Total megatons	
Minuteman II	450	1	450	1.0	450.0	450
Minuteman III	550	3	1,650	0.17	280.5	512
(with MK-12A)	(550)	(3)	(1,650)	(0.35)	(572.5)	(825)
Titan II	54	1	54	9.0	486.0	232
Total ICBMs	1,054		2,154		1,216.5	1,194
					(1,508.5)	(1,507)
Poseidon	336	10	3,360	0.04	134	403
Poseidon C-4	160	8	1,280	0.10	128	282
Trident I	240	8	1,920	0.10	192	422
Total SLBMs	736		6,560		454	1,107
B-52 G/H	165	{ 6 SRAM	990	0.2	198	337
		{ 4 bombs	660	1.0	660	660
B-52CM	165	20 ALCM	3,300	0.2	660	1,122
FB-111	60	{ 2 SRAM	120	0.2	24	41
		{ 2 bombs	120	1.0	120	120
Total bombers	390		5,190		1,662	2,280
Grand total	2,180		13,904		3,332.5	4,581
					(3,629.5)	(4,894)

SOURCE: *Counterforce Issues for the U.S. Strategic Nuclear Forces*, Congressional Budget Office, January 1978.

pabilities of Soviet strategic systems. Consequently, some of the assumptions of the studies used in writing this book are inconsistent. In an analysis of relative U.S. and Soviet military effectiveness, the outcomes of a study would be very sensitive to the exact technical data used. In a study of the impacts of nuclear war on civilian population, however, a small difference in the estimated yield or accuracy of a Soviet weapon will have no corresponding effect on the computation of the consequences of a particular attack.

Estimates of U.S. strategic capability, on the other hand, are not subject to such great uncertainties. The Congressional Budget Office summary of U.S. forces is shown in Table A2.

Note that Soviet ICBM warheads are much higher in yield than their U.S. counterparts. This means that Soviet attacks on U.S. targets will produce much more collateral damage (i.e., population casualties from attacks on economic targets, or economic and population damage from attacks on military targets) than will U.S. attacks on Soviet targets.

Which weapons are used in our attack cases? In Case 1, Detroit is targeted with a single warhead similar to those deployed on the multiple independently targetable reentry vehicle (MIRVed) SS-18 ICBM or with a large single weapon such as those carried by SS-9 or SS-8 Soviet ICBMs. Leningrad is targeted with yields approximately those of a Minuteman II warhead, a Titan II warhead, or all 10 reentry vehicles (RVs) from Poseidon submarine-launched ballistic missiles (SLBM). In the "limited" attacks on oil refineries, the U.S.S.R. attacks U.S. targets with 10 MIRVed SS-18 warheads, and the United States attacks Soviet targets with a mix of Poseidon and Minuteman III missiles, numbering 73 warheads. In the counterforce attacks, each side uses its most accurate MIRVed ICBMs against the other side's silos, and a mix of ICBMs, SLBMs, and bombers against bomber and missile submarine bases.

Notes

Chapter 2. Possible Nuclear Wars

1. *Long-Term Worldwide Effects of Multiple Nuclear Weapons Detonations* (Washington: National Academy of Sciences, 1975).

Chapter 3. The Effects of Nuclear Weapons

1. This scenario considers Detroit to be the only damaged area in the United States. It is assumed that there is no other threat that would prevent survivors and those in surrounding areas from giving all possible aid. It is also assumed that federal and state governments will actively organize outside assistance.
2. Office of Technology Assessment, "Nuclear Proliferation and Safeguards" (Washington: U.S. Government Printing Office, 1977), pp. 121 – 22.

Chapter 4. Civil Defense Measures

1. T. K. Jones, "Industrial Survival and Recovery After Nuclear Attack: A Report to the Joint Committee on Defense Production, U.S. Congress" (Seattle: The Boeing Aerospace Company, 1976).
2. P. T. Egorov, I. A. Shlyakov, and N. I. Alabin, *Civil Defense*. Translated by Scientific Translation Service (Springfield, Virginia: Department of Commerce, National Technical Information Service, 1973), p. 101.
3. Central Intelligence Agency, *Soviet Civil Defense.* (Washington: Director of Central Intelligence, 1978). The text quoted is from pp. 2 – 3.
4. Arms Control and Disarmament Agency, *An Analysis of Civil Defense in Nuclear War* (Washington, D.C.: U.S. Arms Control and Disarmament Agency, 1978).

Chapter 5. Three Nuclear Attack Cases

1. Bill Curry, "Gulf Plants Combed for Carcinogens," *Washington Post*, February 19, 1979, p. A3.
2. "U.S. Refining Capacity" (Washington: National Petroleum Refiners' Association, July 28, 1978), p. 1 (U.S. figures); and *International Petroleum Encyclopedia, 1976* (Tulsa, Oklahoma: Petroleum Publishing Co., 1977), p. 323 (Soviet figures).
3. *International Petroleum Encyclopedia, 1976*, p. 393 (Soviet figures); and "U.S. Refining Capacity," *passim* (U.S. figures).
4. *Statistical Abstract of the United States, 1978* (Washington: U.S. Department of Commerce, Bureau of the Census, 1978), lists 91,846,000 employed persons age 16 and over in the United States, of whom 2,469,000 were listed as farmworkers, for January – April, 1978 (p. 418). The *Statistical Abstract* does not present the amount of petroleum consumed by American agriculture. Several statistics, however, indicate this number to be a small fraction of total U.S. petroleum consumption. Preliminary 1977 data showed all U.S. prime movers (automotive and others) had 26,469 million horsepower, while farms accounted for 328 million horsepower, or 1.2 percent (p. 604). In 1976, industrial consumption of petroleum accounted for 18 percent of total U.S. petroleum consumption (p. 764). And a National Academy of Sciences study found that agriculture accounted for 3.5 percent of total national energy consumption in 1968. *Agricultural Production Efficiency* (Washington: National Academy of Sciences, National Research Council, Committee on Agricultural Production Efficiency, 1975), p. 119.
5. Hedrick Smith, *The Russians* (New York: Ballantine Books, 1977), p. 241.

Chapter 6. Long-Term Effects

1. Editor's note: These conclusions reflect the state of knowledge on the ozone layer as of early 1980, when the OTA report was originally released. As of 1982, it appears that the 1975 NAS study was close to the actual magnitude of the ozone layer depletion, even though its models of the upper atmosphere were in error.

References

General Books on Nuclear War

Adams, Ruth and Susan Cullen, *The Final Epidemic: Physicians and Scientists on Nuclear War*, (Chicago: University of Chicago Press, 1982).

Beres, Louis René, *Apocalypse: Nuclear Catastrophe in World Politics*, (Chicago: University of Chicago Press, 1982).

Calder, Nigel, *Nuclear Nightmares: An Investigation into Possible Wars*, (New York, Viking Press, 1980).

Committee for the Compilation of Materials on the Damage of the Atomic Bombs in Hiroshima and Nagasaki, *Hiroshima and Nagasaki*, translated by Ishikawa and Swain, (New York: Basic Books, 1981).

Ground Zero, *Nuclear War: What's in It for You?* (New York: Pocket Books, 1982).

Hersey, John, *Hiroshima*, (New York: Alfred Knopf, 1946).

Katz, Arthur M., *Life After Nuclear War*, (Cambridge, Massachusetts: Ballinger Publishing Co., 1982).

Osada, Arata, *Children of Hiroshima*, (Cambridge, Massachusetts: Oelgeschlager, Gunn & Hain, 1981).

Rosenberg, Harold, *Atomic Soldiers: American Victims of Nuclear Experiments*, (Boston: Beacon Press, 1980).

Schell, Jonathan, *The Fate of the Earth*, (New York: Alfred Knopf, 1982).

United Nations, *Nuclear Weapons: Report of the Secretary-General*, (Boston: Autumn Press, 1981).

Physical Effects of Nuclear Warfare

Ayers, R.N., "Environmental Effects of Nuclear Weapons" (3 vols.), Hudson Institute Report No. HI-518, December 1965.

Batten, E.S., "The Effects of Nuclear War on the Weather and Climate," RAND Corp., RM-4989, November 1966.

Bennett, B., "Fatality Uncertainties in Limited Nuclear War," RAND Corp., R-2218-AF, November 1977.

Defense Civil Preparedness Agency, U.S. Department of Defense, "DCPA Attack Environment Manual," Publication CPG 2-1A, 9 vols., June 1973 (vol. 4 revised June 1977).

Drell, S. and von Hippel, "Limited Nuclear War," *Scientific American*, November 1976.

Glasstone and Dolen, eds: *Effects of Nuclear Weapons*, 3rd ed., (Washington: U.S. Department of Defense and Department of Energy, 1977).

Green, J., "Response to DCPA Questions on Fallout," Defense Civil Preparedness Agency, Washington, D.C., November 1973.

Mark, J.C., "Global Consequences of Nuclear Weaponry," *Annual Review of Nuclear Science*, 1976, 26:51 – 87.

National Academy of Sciences, "Effects of Multiple Nuclear Explosions Worldwide," Washington, D.C., 1975.

U.S. Arms Control & Disarmament Agency, "The Effects of Nuclear War," Washington, D.C., April 1979.

U.S. Congress, Senate, Committee on Foreign Relations, Subcommittee on Arms Control, International Organizations, and Security Agreements, Comm. Print: "Analyses of Effects of Limited Nuclear Warfare," 94th Cong., 1st sess. (1975).

General Economic Impact of Nuclear War

Goen, R., et al., "Analysis of National Entity Survival," Stanford Research Institute, November 1967.

Goen, R., et al., "Critical Factors Affecting National Survival," Stanford Research Institute, 1965.

Goen, R., et al., "Potential Vulnerabilities Affecting National Survival," Stanford Research Institute, 1970.

Hanunian, N., "Dimensions of Survival: Postattack Survival Disparities and National Viability," RAND Corp., RM-5140, November 1966.

Hirshleiter, J., "Economic Recovery," RAND Corp., P-3160, August 1965.

Katz, A., "Economic and Social Consequences of Nuclear Attacks on the United States," U.S. Senate, Committee on Banking, Housing, and Urban Affairs, 96th Cong., 1st sess. (March 1979).

Laurius, R., and F. Dresch, "National Entity Survival: Measure and Countermeasure," Stanford Research Institute, 1971.

Lee, H., et al., "Industrial Production and Damage Repair Following Nuclear Attack," Stanford Research Institute, March 1968.

Pettis, Dzirbals, Krahenbuhl, "Economic Recovery Following Nuclear Disaster: A Selected, Annotated Bibliography," RAND Corp., R-2143, December 1977.

Sobin, B., "Post Attack Recovery," Research Analysis Corp., RAC-P-51, June 1970.

Winter, S. G., Jr., "Economic Recovery From the Effects of Thermonuclear War," RAND Corp., P-2416, August 1961.

Winter, S. G., Jr., "Economic Viability After Nuclear War: The Limits of Feasible Production," RAND Corp., RM-3436, September 1963.

Specific Economic Impacts of Nuclear War

Brown, S., "Agricultural Vulnerability to Nuclear War," Stanford Research Institute, February 1973.

Jones, T.K., "Industrial Survival and Recovery After Nuclear Attack: A Report to the Joint Committee on Defense Production, U.S. Congress," The Boeing Co., Seattle, Wash., 1976.

Killion, et al., "Effects of Fallout Radiation on Crop Production," Comparative Animal Research Laboratory, July 1975.

Leavitt, J., "Analysis and Identification of Nationally Essential Industries, Vol. I: Theoretical Approach," Institute for Defense Analyses, P-972, March 1974.

Stanford Research Institute, "U.S. Agriculture: Potential Vulnerabilities," January 1969.

Stanford Research Institute, "Agricultural Vulnerability in the National Entity Survival Context," July 1970.

Stephens, M.M., "Vulnerability of Total Petroleum Systems," Office of Oil and Gas, Department of the Interior, May 1973.

Administrative, Social, Psychological Factors

Allmitt, B., "A Study of Consensus on Social and Psychological Factors Related to Recovery From Nuclear Attack," Human Sciences Research, Inc., May 1971.

Brown, W.M., "Emergency Mobilization for Postattack Reorganization," Hudson Institute, HI-874/2, May 1968.

Brown, W.M., "On Reorganizing After Nuclear Attack," RAND Corp., P-3764, January 1968.

Dresch, F., "Information Needs for Post-Attack Recovery Management," Stanford Research Institute, April 1968.

Ellis, Dresche, "Industrial Factors in Total Vulnerability," Stanford Research Institute, April 1968.

Hirshleiter, J., "Disaster and Recovery: A Historical Survey," RAND Corp., RM-3079, April 1963.

Iklé, F. C., The Social Impact of Bomb Destruction, (Norman, Oklahoma: University of Oklahoma Press, 1958).

Janis, I., Air War and Emotional Stress, (New York: McGraw Hill, 1951).

Vestermark, S., (ed.), "Vulnerabilities of Social Structure," Human Sciences Research, Inc., December 1966.

Winter, S. G., Jr., "The Federal Role in Post Attack Economic Organization," P-3737, RAND Corp., November 1967.

Civil Defense

Aspin, Les, "The Mineshaft Gap Revisited," Congressional Record, Jan. 15, 1979, pp. E26 – 35.

Egorov, P.T., et al., Civil Defense, (Springfield, Virginia: National Technical Information Service, 1973). A translation of Grazhdanskaya Oborna, 2nd ed., Moscow, 1970.

Gouré, L., War Survival in Soviet Strategy, (Washington: Advanced International Studies Institute, 1976).

Gouré, L., Soviet Civil Defense in the Seventies, (Washington: Advanced International Studies Institute, 1975).

Kaplan, F. M., "The Soviet Civil Defense Myth: Parts I & II," Bulletin of the Atomic Scientists, March and April 1978.

Kincaid, W., "Repeating History: the Civil Defense Debate Renewed," *International Security,* Winter 1978.

Sullivan, R., et al., "Candidate U.S. Civil Defense Programs," System Planning Corp., March 1978.

Sullivan, R., et al., "Civil Defense Needs of High-Risk Areas of the United States," System Planning Corporation, SPC 409, 1979.

U.S Arms Control and Disarmament Agency, "An Analysis of Civil Defense in Nuclear War," Washington, D.C., December 1978.

U.S. C.I.A., "Soviet Civil Defense," Director of Central Intelligence, NI78-10003, July 1978.

U.S. Congress, Senate, Committee on Banking, Housing, and Urban Affairs, (Hearings on Civil Defense), Jan. 8, 1979.

Glossary

Air Burst. A nuclear weapons explosion that occurs above the ground surface, high enough so that the resulting fireball does not touch the earth or scoop out a crater. See also *surface burst*.

Alpha Particle. A particle emitted spontaneously from unstable nuclei of some radioactive elements. It is identical with a helium nucleus, having four mass units and an electric charge of two positive units. Compared to other forms of radiation at the same energy, it does not have much penetrating power.

Beta Particle. An electron emitted spontaneously from unstable nuclei of some radioactive elements. Depending upon its energy, it can penetrate body tissue fairly deeply and cause substantial damage to internal organs and tissue.

Blast Shelter. A structure, usually embedded in the earth, designed to withstand the overpressures due to a nuclear blast; specifically a shelter that can withstand a 10 psi overpressure. The "hardness" of a blast shelter refers to the level of overpressure it can withstand.

Conflagration. A massive fire that occurs after a nuclear explosion, in which the flames spread along a common front. See also *firestorm*.

Counterforce Attack. A nuclear attack directed solely against the enemy's military targets. See also *countersilo attack*.

Countersilo Attack. A nuclear attack directed solely against hardened ICBM silos and not against other military or economic targets. See also *counterforce attack*.

Crater. The pit, depression or cavity formed in the surface of the earth by a nuclear explosion near ground level. See also *surface burst*.

Crisis Relocation. The evacuation of people from high-risk to low-risk areas during a threat of nuclear attack.

Direct Radiation. The nuclear radiation, composed mainly of gamma rays and neutrons, that occurs immediately at the time of detonation. It is usually very intense, but its range is limited to a few miles around the center of the explosion. Also known as *prompt radiation*.

Dynamic Pressure. The high air pressure that results from mass air flow (or wind) behind the shock front of a blast wave. See also *overpressure*.

Electromagnetic Pulse *(EMP)*. A sharp pulse of radio frequency (long wave-length) electromagnetic radiation produced when a nuclear weapon is detonated at or near the earth's surface, or at high altitudes. The intense electric and magnetic fields that result can damage unprotected electrical and electronic equipment.

Expedient Shelters. Fallout shelters (also known as *hasty shelters*) offering reasonable radiation protection that can be fashioned quickly in the event of nuclear attack. See also *fallout shelter* and *protection factor*.

Fallout. The descent to the Earth's surface of particles contaminated with radioactive material scooped up by a nuclear blast from the earth's surface. The term also applies in a collective sense, to the contaminated particles themselves. Early (or *local*) fallout includes those larger, heavier particles which fall to ground within 24 hours after a nuclear explosion. Delayed (or *global*) fallout consists of the smaller particles that ascend into the stratosphere and are carried by winds to all parts of the Earth. This delayed fallout is brought to earth, mainly by rain and snow, over extended periods ranging from months to years.

Fallout Shelter.   A structure designed to protect its inhabitants against the effects of radioactive fallout. Generally, it will have thick walls and roof to attenuate nuclear radiation, plus provisions for air filtration, food, water, etc. See also *fallout* and *protection factor.*

Firestorm.   A stationary, massive fire that occurs after a nuclear explosion, in which violent inrushing winds create extremely high temperatures but prevent the fire from spreading outwards. See also *conflagration.*

Fission.   A nuclear reaction in which heavy atomic nuclei — usually uranium or plutonium — are split into lighter nuclei, releasing tremendous amounts of energy and radiation. See also *fusion.*

Fission Products.   A general term for the complex mixture of substances produced as a result of nuclear fission. Something like 80 different fission fragments result from roughly 40 different modes of fission of a given nuclear species (e.g., uranium-235 or plutonium-239). These 80 fragments, being mostly radioactive, immediately begin to decay, forming additional *(daughter)* products, with the result that the complex mixture so formed contains over 300 different isotopes of 36 elements. See also *fission.*

Flashblindness.   A temporary blindness, lasting up to several minutes, that results in people who are looking in the direction of a nuclear explosion at the instant of detonation.

Footprint.   The total area within which the individual warheads originating from a single missile can be aimed.

Fuel Loading.   The density of flammable materials (usually measured in lb/ft^2 or kg/m^2) occurring in the area subject to a nuclear blast. Typical figures are 2 lb/ft^2 in U.S. suburbs and 5 lb/ft^2 in urban neighborhoods. The ignition of a firestorm is thought to require a fuel loading of 8 lb/ft^2. See also *conflagration* and *firestorm.*

Fusion.   A nuclear reaction in which two very light atomic nuclei, usually isotopes of hydrogen, combine to form a heavier nucleus, releasing tremendous amounts of energy and radiation. See also *fission.*

Gamma Rays.   High-energy electromagnetic radiation originating from decaying atomic nuclei. They have very high penetrating power and can be extremely damaging to body tissues.

Groud Zero.   The point on the earth's surface directly beneath the center of the nuclear fireball, in the case of an air burst. In the case of a surface burst, ground zero refers to the exact center of the nuclear fireball at the instant of detonation.

Height of Burst (HOB).   The height above the earth's surface at which a bomb is detonated in the air. The optimum height of burst for a particular target is the height at which a weapon of specified energy will produce a certain desired effect over the maximum possible area.

Ionizing Radiation.   High-energy nuclear radiation, such as alpha and beta particles and gamma rays, that can penetrate bodily tissues and cause damage by ionizing the atoms (that is, by knocking electrons out of these atoms) along its path. See also *nuclear radiation.*

Infrared Radiation.   Invisible electromagnetic radiation much like visible light but with a longer wavelength and lower energy. Almost half the energy in sunlight comes as infrared radiation of a slightly longer wavelength than visible light. A large portion of the "heat radiation" from a nuclear blast is infrared radiation.

Kiloton (kt).   An equivalent amount of energy released in a nuclear explosion that is approximately equal to that released in the explosion of 1,000 tons (1 kiloton) of TNT.

Megaton (Mt).   An equivalent amount of energy released in a nuclear explosion that is approximately equal to that released in the explosion of 1 million tons (1 megaton) of TNT.

Neutron.   A neutral nuclear particle of unit mass that is present in all atomic nuclei except hydrogen. Large numbers of neutrons are produced by both fission and fusion reactions in nuclear explosions.

Nuclear Radiation.   The particles and electromagnetic radiation emitted from atomic nuclei in various nuclear processes. All nuclear radiations, which include alpha particles, beta particles, gamma rays and neutrons, are ionizing radiation that can damage body tissues. See also *alpha particle, beta particle, gamma ray* and *neutron.*

Overpressure.   The transient air pressure, usually expressed in pounds per square inch (psi), exceeding the normal outdoor air pressure that is manifested in the shock (or blast) wave from a nuclear explosion. The *peak overpressure* is the maximum value of the overpressure that occurs at the particular location, and is generally experienced at the instant the shock wave reaches that location. See also *dynamic pressure.*

Ozone Layer.   A region of the Earth's atmosphere,

about 20 to 30 miles above the surface, characterized by high levels of ozone (O_3). This layer absorbs most of the ultraviolet radiation present in sunlight in outer space, protecting living cells from its harmful effects.

Prompt Effects. Effects of nuclear explosions that occur immediately after detonation, in contrast to later effects, such as fallout, ozone layer depletion, etc.

Protection Factor (PF). The reduction in levels of nuclear radiation, from outdoor levels to those inside a fallout shelter, that can be achieved by a particular selection and thickness of shielding materials. For example, a protection factor of 10 will reduce the inside level of radiation to one-tenth of that experienced just outside.

Rad. A unit of the dose of radiation absorbed that represents the absorption of 100 ergs of nuclear (or ionizing) radiation per gram of absorbing material, such as body tissue. See also *rem* and *roentgen*.

Rem. A unit of biological dose of radiation absorbed by a human being. The number of rems of radiation is equal to the number of rads absorbed multiplied by the relative biological effectiveness of the particular type of radiation (e.g., gamma rays, alpha particles, neutrons). The rem is also the unit of dose equivalent, which is equal to the product of the number of rads absorbed and the "quality factor" of the radiation. See also *rad* and *roentgen*.

Roentgen. A unit of exposure to gamma (or X) radiation. An exposure of 1 roentgen results in the deposition of about 94 ergs or energy in 1 gram of soft body tissue. Thus, an exposure of 1 roentgen is approximately equivalent to an absorbed dose of 1 rad in soft tissue. See also *rad* and *rem*.

Surface Burst. A nuclear weapons explosion that occurs on or near the earth's surface; the resulting fireball will usually scoop out a crater in the earth. See also *air burst*.

Thermal Radiation. The electromagnetic radiation (as distinct from gamma rays) emitted from the fireball because of its very high temperature. It consists mainly of ultraviolet, visible, and infrared radiation. In the early stages, when the fireball temperature is extremely high, the ultraviolet radiation predominates. Later, the fireball temperatures are lower and most of the thermal radiation lies in the visible and infrared regions of the spectrum.

Ultraviolet Radiation. Invisible electromagnetic radiation much like visible light but of a shorter wavelength and higher energy. Most ultraviolet radiation in sunlight is absorbed by the ozone layer of the earth's atmosphere.

GUIDE TO ACRONYMNS

ACDA Arms Control and Disarmament Agency
BEIR Biological Effects of Ionizing Radiation
CB Citizen's Band
CIA Central Intelligence Agency
DCPA Defense Civil Preparedness Agency
DOD Department of Defense
EBS Emergency Broadcast System
EMP ElectroMagnetic Pulse
EOC Emergency Operating Center
FDAA Federal Disaster Assistance Administration
FEMA Federal Emergency Management Agency
FPA Federal Preparedness Agency
FY Fiscal Year
HOB Height Of Burst
ICBM InterContinental Ballistic Missile
MIRV Multiple Independently-targetable Reentry Vehicles
NAS National Academy of Sciences
NATO North American Treaty Organization
OTA Office of Technology Assessment
FP Protection Factor
RV Reentry Vehicle
SALT Strategic Arms Limitation Talks
SLBM Submarine-Launched Ballistic Missile
SNDV Strategic Nuclear Delivery Vehicle

Index

THE DAY AFTER MIDNIGHT
was designed by Wendy Calmenson,
with copy editing and proofreading by R. G. Beukers,
art direction and production by Meredith Ittner,
and index by Elinor Lindheimer.
The text was set in VIP Melior by Innovative Media,
the paper is P & S Finch Offset Vellum,
and the book was printed and bound by Malloy Lithographing
of Ann Arbor, Michigan.